BONES BENEATH THE PRAIRIE

A Memoir of Survival and Redemption

ROSEANN MAYER

Published by Roseann Mayer

ISBN: 979-8-9997895-0-1

First Edition, 2025
Printed in the United States of America

Bones Beneath the Prairie is a memoir of survival, love, and redemption.

TABLE OF CONTENTS

DEDICATION

To the Ones Who Stood in the Gap
—EZEKIEL 22:30

I set out to write about Albany—the land, the legacy, the laughter.
But the harder truths rose too, and the Spirit would not let me
leave them out. *Not for vengeance. Not for pity.* But so that
someone still in the dark might see light.

This is a love letter.
To the land that shaped me.
To the God who carried me.
To the family and friends who prayed me through.

For my parents—whose gifts of beauty, tradition, and love remain in me.
For KM—who walked through fire and loved me back to life.
For my children—this was never meant to wound, but to shine a light.
For KM's family, who welcomed me as their own.
For our grandchildren—you are the joy set before me.
For DLR, whose prayers never ceased.
And for MM, whose love was always steady and sure.

If you are weary or walking through fire, remember:
His love is already there, waiting to catch you.

—RM.

FOREWORD

There are some stories that don't just speak—they testify.
This one does.

*B*ones Beneath the Prairie is more than a memoir. It is a witness. A testimony of survival, grace, and the kind of quiet strength that only comes from walking through fire with the Lord at your side.

I have known Roseann for many years, both as a sister in Christ and through my work in ministry. I have watched her walk through seasons of deep sorrow and surprising strength. What I know of her is not performative faith, but faith lived—honest, sometimes trembling, but enduring.

This book is not easy reading, nor is it meant to be. It is raw, real, and ultimately redemptive. Roseann writes for the daughters who were taught to be silent, the wives who bore their suffering in secret, and the women who long for the courage to tell the truth and still cling to God.

There is power in a testimony like this. There is healing in it.

As a pastoral counselor, I believe this book will minister to many. Not because Roseann claims to have answers, but because she dares to tell the truth—with humility, with grace, and with a love that points beyond herself to the One who carried her.

You don't have to know her to feel the weight of her story. You will know it when it reaches your spirit. This is a book for all who have lived through quiet storms and still reach for the light.

May her courage become your invitation.

—JIMMY R. MCLEOD, D.MIN., M.DIV., M.A., BCPC
BOARD CERTIFIED PASTORAL COUNSELOR

PREFACE

This is my story, told as truthfully as I know how—a journey through the shadows of domestic violence into the uncertain light of faith and healing. Memory is imperfect. It holds the ache as much as the fact. What you'll find here is not a precise record of dates and details, but the lived truth that shaped me.

To protect my children, grandchildren, and others, I have changed names, locations, and some details. Certain events are compressed or reordered, but the heart remains: the emotional truth of survival, my West Texas roots, and the grace of God that carried me through.

I did not come through blameless. I stayed when I should have left, clung to illusions, and excused what should never have been excused. This story carries those mistakes alongside the wounds—because pretending otherwise would be another kind of lie.

Domestic violence is not always broken glass or flashing lights. More often it hides in the quiet—the clink of silverware, the silence when the phone rings, the glance that warns you to stay still. It hides in houses where neighbors wave and believe all is well.

Statistics say one in three women will endure violence from a partner. But numbers don't tell you how it feels to wait for footsteps, heart pounding, certain they are coming for you. This book is my attempt to give those silences a voice. Some scenes may be difficult for those who know me, but they remain because silence helps no one. Survivors deserve to see their truth on the page.

It is for the woman still in the smoke, for the child listening for safety, for anyone who needs to know: you are not alone.

This is my offering—to the girl I was, to the woman I became, and to the God who never let me go.

Turn the page, and walk with me.

PROLOGUE

This is a story about what time leaves behind—the bones that never quite stop rattling beneath the prairie floor of a family and a town. Memory doesn't slip away; it bruises. It buries itself. It curls up in the dark like a secret child, waiting for you to find it again.

Mine used to be vivid. Bright. Full of Kodachrome slides: Miss Thelma hanging white sheets on a clothesline, the wooden snap of clothespins in the wind; Sunday cake cooling on the counter, its vanilla-sugar scent thick in the air; the creak of a screen door; starched dresses so stiff you could stand them in the corner.

I remember the sound of cicadas droning in August; the heat shimmering above blacktop; the way the prairie sky stretched so far it made you dizzy if you looked too long. Albany was oil rigs on the horizon and cattle in the pastures, but also Sunday sermons where everybody knew your mother's laugh and your father's handshake. Respectability mattered. People noticed what shoes you wore to church, who you sat beside, and whether you kept your troubles private.

Lately, I reached for those things and felt them dissolve—like a name I almost remembered, or the scent of someone who once brushed my hair after church. They were fragments of a self I wasn't sure I'd ever see again, tethered to a red-leather photo album Mom had stitched for me as a college keepsake. Gold-embossed, heavy in the lap, it held the best parts of me—the real me, the happy me. A reminder of home, of who I could be if I reclaimed it. Sometimes I'd run my hand across its cover the way you touch a Bible, reverent, almost afraid to open. Inside were pictures of me at Baylor, short hair cut in the style of the day, a green wool turtleneck paired with checked pants that made me feel grown up and worldly. I can still see one photo of me laughing at a football game, sunlight across my cheek, as if I had never once been touched by sorrow.

But my marriage had been a firestorm from the very beginning. Not the kind that warms a cold room, but the kind that devours walls, beams, and anything nailed down. At first, I mistook the heat for passion. He was older, worldly in a way that thrilled me after years of strict rules. He pulled me out of my parents' orbit, out of their iron insistence on propriety, and I confused that freedom with love. But fire consumes what it touches. By the summer of 1982, in the thick West Texas heat—an era when a woman's silence was often her only shield against the storm—I was thirty-two, married nearly seven years, with a fifteen-month-old son and another baby swelling my belly. That fire had consumed enough. It was time to escape—and maybe, over the decades ahead, unearth those buried memories like a lifeline, piecing together a life that spanned fifty years of hidden battles and hard-won freedoms.

Part 1:
What I Left Behind

That afternoon, I confronted him about something—I can't even recall the exact words now, only that I had the truth. Whatever the subject was, I knew it down to my bones. And he had a con, a story spun to cover the rot. When his cover cracked, the mask dropped.

He slapped me.

The sound was louder than it should have been—a sharp, flat, crack that echoed off the walls. My head snapped sideways, and I stumbled to the floor. The carpet scratched my palms. Before I could catch my breath, he was on me, yanking me up by the arm. The bruise bloomed immediately under his fingers—a hot, aching band that would stay for days.

Somewhere in the house, the baby started crying.

His fury sucked the air out of the room. My ears rang. My cheek throbbed, the metallic tang of blood mixing with the bitter aftertaste of humiliation. And then—just as fast—he let go. He stormed out the front door, the front slamming against its frame, and I stood there, dizzy, hearing his old clunker cough to life in the driveway. The sound of him peeling away wasn't freedom, but it was my only opening.

I hadn't seen the fire-y tornado coming at first. Back in '77, I met him on a job interview for his shop—he hired me on the spot, a mysterious shopkeeper from a different social class, nine years my senior, with a sensual edge I'd never encountered at twenty-two. He was in the middle of a divorce, sparked by a mistress in another city, and his goal was sex, not commitment, while he juggled her and others. I knew nothing of his sexual addiction then, pushing for a genuine relationship even as he kept his secrets. But within months, I witnessed the storm: his lady friend called; I answered and boldly claimed our involvement.

When he found out, he slapped me, ripping a solid gold watch from my wrist and twisting it into a mangled heap on the floor. I should have run then—God knows why I didn't—but I pursued him with all my vigor, escaping my strict parents' control and their iron grip on respectability. We married in '78; he didn't want it, didn't love me, but I needed the ring to justify our intimacy, to escape lectures on no sex before marriage, my parents' disapproval of my rebellious life choices, and their obsession with appearances. Women like me didn't question a ring as escape. But the slaps started small, fueled by his own buried rage, and hidden by my inexperience: in all my life, I had never seen a man lay a hand on a woman, so I had no language for what was happening to me.

Time had no edges. Logic had no foothold. Only motion mattered. I was leaving.

Shoes. Diapers. My keys. The baby.

That's all I remember throwing into the car—not neatly, not carefully—just whatever I could grab with one hand while the other clutched my son tight. He was fifteen months old, feverish, curls damp with sweat. His sippy cup clattered to the concrete driveway when I missed the open mouth of the diaper bag. I left it there. No time to bend. No time for anything but out.

Seven months pregnant, my belly was hard with panic. She kicked as I slammed the door and turned the ignition, her little body shifting inside me like she already knew: we were leaving for good.

This wasn't bravery. I hadn't calculated the risk. It was survival—pure, breathless survival. But in that moment, I chose it deliberately, whispering to myself, This ends now. For them. For me.

I didn't check the stove. The red-leather photo album never crossed my mind—that tether to my past, now left behind like so much ash. One day, I'd rebuild those memories, stitch them back together. But not today.

I turned the wheel and headed for the open road—not because I knew where I was going, but because I knew where I wasn't staying. The baby whimpered in the back seat, rubbing his fists into his eyes. I reached for him at every stoplight, brushing his toes with my fingertips, whispering it was going to be okay even though my pulse told me it might not be.

I kept glancing in the rearview, half-expecting to see headlights gaining on me. Every corner I turned, every block I put between us, I waited for him to come roaring around the bend.

But I kept driving.

PART 2:
THE LINE IN THE SAND

I won't name him here. He doesn't deserve it. Not because I'm afraid—though I was, for far too long—but because naming him gives him shape. He isn't at the center of this story. Just the tremor that cracked it open—his own fractures from childhood and hardship spilling into our life, turning promises to poison over the years.

This was my peak: where I cried *halt*.

I pulled off the highway and parked behind a budget motel, the kind with sun-bleached curtains and a flickering neon sign that buzzed like a warning. It smelled of stale smoke and regret. I carried only the diaper bag, my purse, and one overnight bag. No toys. No stroller. I was present, but for a short duration. I had maybe three days if I stretched the cash.

The woman at the front desk didn't ask questions. She wore a polyester vest with a crooked name tag, "Darlene"—and smelled like cigarettes and quiet endurance. I apologized for how I must've looked and told her I'd be staying alone for a few days. She didn't blink, just slid the key across the counter with a knowing glance. Another one, her eyes seemed to say. I wonder now how many women like me she'd checked in—eyes tired, voices thin, bruises hidden under sleeves. Maybe she'd been one herself once, spotting the signs in every weary shuffle through that lobby.

Inside the room, the baby was restless from the heat, from the confusion, from me. He didn't understand why his mother's arms shook, why she jumped at every sound. He wanted only his bottle and his familiar crackers. But he stayed close, curling into my chest like a heartbeat I could still hold on to—his tiny fingers tangled in the hem of my shirt, an anchor like the forgotten photo album, pulling me toward some reclaimed self.

I stayed two nights. Fed the baby. Hid in the bathroom to cry. Stacked towels against the base of the door so the hallway light couldn't slip in. Watched the shadows beneath it like they might become men. And in those heavy silences, I asked myself the question I had avoided for years: How had it gotten this far? When had I stopped believing I could leave, or that I deserved more?

The answers hung in the stagnant air. I prayed. I cursed. I whispered escape routes to the popcorn ceiling. Every car in the lot made me freeze. Every voice outside felt like a warning. I left the television on low-volume news—just enough to drown the unraveling quiet.

He had been driving all over town for two days, never dreaming I'd hole up here. I'd parked the car in the shadowed end of the lot, half-hidden by a sagging chain-link fence. There was no bus, no taxi—this was West Texas, where a car was your only lifeline—so mine came with me, risk and all. Still, he found me.

The banging came first. Fist on metal. Foot against wood.

"OPEN THE DOOR."

His voice cracked like a rifle shot.

"YOU CAN'T DO THIS."

I didn't move. I sat on the floor, knees drawn to my chest, the baby cradled in my arms. The pounding rattled the frame. The deadbolt held, but the sound splintered through me.

Then the pleading. The bargaining.

"I know I screwed everything up, but don't shut me out. I can fix this. I will fix this. Just let me talk to you—please. You can't take my son."

The pounding shifted—urgent, violent. His foot struck harder. The metal frame shrieked. The handle jumped.

This was the hinge: threat turning to breaking. The air tightened around my chest.

Then—silence. Worse than yelling. More dangerous.

I reached for the rotary phone. I could have called 911. But I didn't. In '82, I didn't know who to call or where to turn. No one had ever told me what to do if a husband crossed that line. So I called my daddy instead.

A beat later I heard it: the slam of a familiar rickety car door, the angry grind of gears, and the tires shrieking as he tore out of the lot. The sound rattled the thin motel walls, then faded into nothing.

When Daddy came, he didn't come alone. Jim was with him—my father's best friend, a tall man with silver hair combed straight back and the quiet gravity of someone who'd faced his own storms. They'd been friends for decades, prominent in the community, the kind who could open doors or close them forever. There was a gravity in Jim's eyes, a steady kind of sorrow, but when he looked at me it softened into something protective, almost fatherly, as if he had claimed me as his own.

I could smell the fury on them before they knocked—in their tight jaws, their side-by-side stance in the flickering doorway.

When I opened the door, Daddy's eyes swept over me—my face, the baby on my hip—and met mine. He nodded once.

"Let's go."

No questions. No lectures. Just command.

Jim took the overnight bag, murmuring, "You're safe now." Daddy took the baby, settling him into the car seat with quiet efficiency.

I slid into the front seat of the Cadillac. Jim closed my door, and when they both climbed in, the silence in that car was its own kind of shield. We didn't talk, not with words. They didn't need the backstory. They had seen enough.

The road out of that parking lot felt like a lifeline, smooth and stretching into the unknown. For the first time in years, I could breathe—deep, unshaken breaths. The baby's fingers still clutched my shirt in sleep, a reminder that memory, like survival, could be reclaimed. One fragment at a time—across the fifty years that would follow, turning silence into strength.

CHAPTER 1:

THE SPARK BEFORE THE SILENCE

—◆—◇—◆—

BONES BENEATH THE PRAIRIE
Roseann Mayer

For a moment, I let myself remember who I was before the silence fell—the girl with sunburned shoulders and a head full of dreams. The one who laughed loud, dreamed wide, and carried a light that refused to dim, even in the shadows that would come.

I needed to hold on to her now.

Before the breaking, before the silence and shame, before the long road out—I was someone. The girl with red Kool-Aid on her upper lip and dirt on her knees from Red Rover games. The one who played "Für Elise" from memory while her dog howled along. She knew the sting of 1950s hairspray holding a beehive against West Texas wind, the taste of Sunday pot roast, the hum of cicadas fueling dreams of faraway cities with her name in lights.

I had a name, though you won't find it here. Not because I'm hiding, but because this story is bigger than one name. It's about all of us who shrank to survive. Who stayed too long. And those who finally left.

I was born in a town so small it fit in your back pocket, its roots tangled deep. We measured time in harvests and Friday night lights, in radio songs over drives past windmills and pump jacks. My people—grandfathers on both sides—worked the oil and land for generations, their faces etched by sun, clothes carrying the scent of crude and cattle.

My grandmother's Bible sat on a polished cedar table, marked with pencil notes and folded bulletins. She taught Sunday School until arthritis bent her fingers, but her voice never quavered when she recited Psalms. From her, I learned how to measure flour for pies without a recipe, how to iron pillowcases until they crackled, how to speak softly in rooms where men held sway.

In that world, a girl was expected to be polite and pleasing. To cook. To keep. To carry silence like a badge of honor. But I was never very good at silence.

I was fierce—loud, chatty, mouthy—the girl who gripped the wheel through skids and laughed off storms. I devoured books by flashlight, scribbled stories in notebook margins, imagined worlds beyond. I studied people, their little tells and exits, memorizing them the way other girls memorized love songs. Dirt roads and hymns shaped me—by grief and grace, by the ache of unspoken wants.

On Sunday afternoons I played the piano. I was barefoot, the sunlight filtering through the window, warming my legs. I'd sing show tunes, hymns, and pop songs when I was alone—pretending a stage in some distant city where crowds clapped for me. The mantel mirror was my first audience, reflecting a girl who believed applause was her birthright.

It started even earlier, at four years old, when Albany's Fort Griffin Fandangle pulled me onto the stage as a tiny Comanche infant—dressed in moccasins, leather with beads, a feather in my hair. I toddled across with a papier-mâché cactus bigger than me, the audience clapping and laughing at us tots. That rush hooked me instantly. From then on, I longed for that spotlight, that belonging.

In school, I sneaked Mom's lipstick, clipped on costume jewelry at recess, strutted in forbidden heels—owning the world. Bossy, talkative, I stirred mischief for laughs. One teacher noted in my yearbook, "You'll run the world or end up in detention—again."

By high school, I was voted Most Obnoxious in a class of 750, wearing it like a crown. Not because I wanted to annoy, but because I wanted to be seen. I chased applause, dared boys, scribbled heartbreaks into hidden notebooks. I dreamed of New York or Nashville but clung to West Texas red dirt—the sunsets, winds, the pull of home amid the wanting.

I was a contradiction: obedient yet rebellious, nurturing yet wild. I'd bake your birthday cake then steal your crush. I carried others' pain as penance, loved deeply, forgave easily—believing I could fix the broken if I tried hard enough.

Then came the years that stripped the sparkle, one edge at a time. When mirrors forgot me. Silence invaded my songs; my laugh turned foreign. I tucked myself into unopened drawers, telling myself it was practicality, not surrender. I didn't know survival could mimic defeat. That fear-twisted love-built cages. That the bright girl would question her own light.

But she was real. I was real. Buried beneath the silence, whispering, waiting.

This is who walks with you now—not just a woman rebuilding, but a girl in a West Texas pasture, arms outstretched, believing the world waited. She prayed aloud, dreamed in color, loved fiercely—even when it broke her.

She's here. In every line.

Listen: her hope, heart, hallelujah.

Not victim. Not ghost.

Survivor. Soul reclaimed.

A voice rising—strong, steady, full of grace.

CHAPTER 2:

THE RETURN TO ALBANY

BONES BENEATH THE PRAIRIE
Roseann Mayer

Back to reality, it was the summer of 1982, I was living back under my parents' roof, fragile and raw from all I had left behind. They insisted a trip to Albany would be good for me—a family wedding, woven into the same weekend as the Fandangle. I said yes, not because I felt safe, but because some part of me longed for the familiar rhythm of home. A thread of tradition, even if it stung, was better than the silence that had become my days.

❧ INTERLUDE—BRIEF INTERMISSION

Albany, Texas, is more than a place—it's the pulse beneath my skin, the dust in the wind, the stories my bones know by heart.

The courthouse rises from the square in proud local limestone, in a quarry just minutes away, its clock tower watching over cracked earth and wide skies. Mesquites dot the prairie, green against sun-bleached grass, rooted deep against wind and drought. Drilling rigs and pumpjacks nod alongside grazing Herefords, barbed-wire fences marking the town's dual lifeblood: oil and cattle.

This was where I learned to belong—in parades, Fandangle rehearsals, elementary Nativity plays where I shone, and summer nights of fireflies and cut-grass scent, the universe humming with possibility.

Every June, for over eighty-five years, the Fort Griffin Fandangle transforms the prairie west of town into living history—a musical pageant where over 250 locals become Plains Indians, soldiers, and settlers. Covered wagons rumble, longhorns thunder, riders gallop, weaving tales of heroism, hardships, humor, and humility under the stars. Outsiders might doubt the name, but here it's real—the dust, music, communal breath until curtain fall.

Now, as the sun rises low and the car hums, that certainty feels distant, like a star through storm clouds. I'm not the girl dancing in gingham anymore. I'm a woman bruised beyond skin, carrying two lives: my fifteen-month-old toddler and the baby I'm carrying.

In the backseat, I was barefoot and swaddled in an old sweatshirt, I hold my son close—his thumb wet, eyes heavy with sleep, his breaths a fragile anchor.

The car holds a quiet anticipation. My mother hums a half-forgotten tune, her calm veiling excitement for the wedding and Fandangle—her voice trembling with hope this trip might mend us. My father drives, focused, jaw tight, knuckles white on the wheel. His silence is a shield for fears he doesn't name.

The AC hums under FM radio crackle—Sinatra weaving nostalgia through scents of coffee, leather, and old tobacco. Beyond the window, mesquites bend in the wind, a hawk circles above, and the horizon wavers with heat.

This land has witnessed my family's generations. The courthouse clock has ticked since 1883, through joy and sorrow. As a child, I sat on its warm steps watching parades, music swirling like promise.

I glance at my son, his fingers curling my sleeve in sleep. My heart aches with protectiveness and weariness. Does he sense the tangled tension, the hope we carry into this homecoming?

As Albany nears, the skyline emerges—low stone houses, church steeples among mesquites, courthouse luminous. For a moment, I'm a girl in gingham again, clutching Mother's hand, inhaling popcorn and asphalt amid brass band cheers.

We turn; Gran's house appears. Creamy stone catches light, ivy climbing wild against order. Gravel crunches; the porch light flickers like a beacon.

The door opens before we stop.

Gran waits—small, poised, radiating strength. White hair swept up, pink blouse pressed. She doesn't ask; she sees. She gathers what I can't say, lifts my son, and he curls into her as if home.

"You'll sleep in the front room," she breathes. "The Pack 'n Play is ready."

No one mentions my fading bruises. Rumors have spun for years—half-truths everyone knows—making silence heavier than questions.

Inside smells of lemon polish and Estée Lauder—tradition, safety. Memories echo in the dust on furniture, laughter from better days. The baby grand waits in the corner for "Sweet Hour of Prayer."

I drift like a ghost past velvet chairs, crystal ashtrays, framed portraits of old weddings. In the guest room, turquoise silk bedspreads and paneled drapes hold their shape. A pink velvet stool sits under a French Provincial mirror. The playpen stands ready, blanket folded.

Water waits on the nightstand.

I sink onto the bed, hand on belly, pressing for ground. Outside, the Cadillac cools.

I don't know whether I'm safe. I don't know what tomorrow holds.

Bruised, breathless, swollen and tired from the pregnancy and running after my toddler and barely stitched together—I snuggle into memories of better times. For a moment, it feels like home.

CHAPTER 3:

WAKING UP AT GRAN'S

BONES BENEATH THE PRAIRIE
Roseann Mayer

Pale light filtered through the lace, a soft insistence that didn't ask, just showed up. I lay still, letting the hush of Gran's house settle around me—the way a place can cradle you even when you know it's borrowed. The air held a thick, respectful quiet, the kind that clings to every hallway and the edge of a doily.

I pulled the quilt under my chin and stared at the plaster ceiling, tracing the hairline cracks like roadmaps I'd walked a hundred times. My chest felt hollow, as if my ribs had creaked open in the night and let all the courage spill out. The ceiling fan turned lazily, its chain clicking against the glass globe with each revolution. Somewhere beyond the walls, a mourning dove called from the telephone wire, its low, throaty song stitching itself into the silence.

Down the hall, my mother spoke in that practiced, polished register she saved for garden clubs and baby showers. She was talking to my son as if everything were fine. As if I hadn't wept into Gran's quilt just hours before. As if I weren't unraveling in slow motion behind closed doors in a house that used to be sanctuary.

Her voice offered no comfort. It offered a reminder: keep it together, keep it quiet, keep moving.

I folded my feet to the floor. Cold. Steady. I dressed quietly, combed my damp hair with my fingers, and walked barefoot through the house. Past the portraits, the piano, the heavy velvet chairs. No good mornings. No coffee. The air smelled faintly of furniture polish, old hymnals, and biscuits cooked yesterday. Every room held memories like breath: Gran humming, Daddy clearing his throat, my cousins racing through the hall. But now, the house was careful, as if it too was bracing itself not to speak too loudly.

"I'm going to take a short drive," I said from the doorway.

My mother barely lifted her gaze from the coffee cup. "Don't be long," she answered. "People will ask where you are."

Of course they would. Because if there was one thing she hated more than disorder, it was explaining it.

The keys waited in the tray by the back door. I stepped outside into the bright, cloudless air. The Cadillac was under the carport, chrome gleaming as stubbornly as ever. It was the car he'd driven to oil leases, funerals, and Friday night football games, the one that had pulled us to Dairy Queen for dipped cones when no one felt like cooking. I opened the door and slid into the familiar weight of the leather, the way it held its shape like an old promise.

It smelled like him. Tobacco and leather and some old-school aftershave I had never known by name. The steering wheel pressed into my palms with a weight that felt like a signal: you don't have to unravel here.

I didn't have a destination. Just the need to move.

I eased out of the driveway and turned left, past the lanterns, past the stone gates, past all the words I couldn't voice. The baby was safe with my mother. My sister hadn't surfaced yet, which somehow roared louder than if she had. And the town—every window watching with polite restraint—made it feel like I wore a target.

But behind the wheel of my father's Cadillac, I could be alone. I could breathe. I could remember who I was before bruises and head-lines and whispered phone calls. Before I became a story told in some-one else's voice.

The road stretched out, two ribbons of sun-bleached pavement between dry mesquite and rusted fence posts. I drove on memory and muscle—the lane markers becoming a rhythm I could trust. The high school football field appeared on my right, its bleachers bleached and splintered by years of August sun. I slowed, remembering Friday nights when the whole town gathered—horns blaring, girls in satin jackets, my father in the stands chewing peanuts, slow and steady.

Next came the Malt Shop, still sagging against the highway, its windows fogged with grease and memory. I could almost taste the chipped mugs of coffee, the fried-egg sandwiches, the way my sister and I had once split a piece of pie paid for with nickels and dimes we'd begged from Daddy's coin purse.

I passed the Baptist church with the steep concrete steps to the sanctuary, the same one where I'd once stood in itchy lace socks while my mother pressed my hair into curls that defied gravity. Vacation Bible School, Christmas pageants, hymns sung off-key. Those steps had felt like the entire world once. Now they looked small, fragile, like a stage for a play I no longer belonged in.

I didn't stop. I couldn't.

The Cadillac hummed along, windows open, hot wind tangling my hair. And as the town gave way to pasture, I let myself remember—not just the landmarks but the girl I had been moving through them.

One summer afternoon I had walked barefoot to the Rexall drug-store, saving pennies to buy a cherry phosphate. The air-conditioning whooshed when I pushed through the door, and the red swivel stools spun lazily at the counter. I'd felt glamorous just ordering, as if the soda jerk might mistake me for a movie star. That girl still lived inside me somewhere, her knees scabbed, her heart wide open.

Soon, I found a dirt road leading toward the lake. We'd called it a lake, but it was really a glorified stock tank—wide, muddy in summer, shallow by design. To us, it had been an ocean. We'd dragged canoes through reeds, told ourselves stories of sunken treasure, dared each other to jump from the dock that groaned like a tired old man beneath us.

I parked in the shade of a live oak and turned off the engine. Silence pressed in, a soft insistence. I stepped out, gravel biting at my heels, and walked to the water's edge.

The air smelled of sun-warmed cedar and dry earth. Dragonflies skimmed the surface, their wings catching light like stained glass. Somewhere in the brush, a grasshopper clicked its wings, and the sound carried like a prayer.

I sat on the edge of the dock and dangled my feet above the water. My reflection shivered, thin and wavering, a version of me I barely recognized. New lines around my eyes. A hollow space behind the gaze. I looked like a woman who'd held her breath for far too long.

I closed my eyes and tried to remember when I'd felt safe in my skin. Maybe here. Or maybe that was a story I told so often it had felt like memory.

Once, years ago, I'd stood on this dock, barefoot, in cutoffs, hair wild from the wind, and shouted into the sky just to hear the echo. It felt like a prayer. A declaration. I'd believed the world was waiting for me, that I would do something grand, something lasting. I didn't yet know how quickly those dreams could be traded for survival. Or for silence.

The wind picked up, rustling the tall grass behind me. I hugged my knees closer and rocked, like a child soothing herself to sleep. Out there on the lake's edge, the silence opened a door, and my thoughts slipped through it.

Sitting there quietly, I thought about my tiny son. His small hands on the edge of Gran's table. His syrup-slick cheeks pressed against her linen. His wide eyes already too wise for a toddler's face. I'd brought him here for safety, but even in this quiet place he could feel the tremor beneath my skin.

Children always know. They smell fear, even when you fold it into pancakes or lullabies.

My thoughts wandered to my mother, slipping into honeyed tones and polite performance, the same hand that had shaken me awake then offering sugar and smiles as if nothing had cracked the surface.

My sister's absence rang louder than any spoken word. We'd been estranged since childhood. The intense dislike of each other was obvious to anyone within three miles of us. The space she'd left wasn't empty—it was sharp-edged, heavy with implication, crowded with a silence that watched from a distance.

And Gran. Steady, constant Gran, moving through the house like a soft breeze you notice only when it lifts the curtain. Her presence wasn't loud; it was felt in every careful detail: the spoons stacked just so; the lavender tucked into the dresser drawers; the porch swing that shifted, as if remembering someone.

Gran said little, but she filled the spaces others left bare. Her love lived in the scent of pound cake cooling on the counter, the folded pillowcases, the cursive notes kept in drawers that still smelled faintly of rosewater and starch.

If I walked into the kitchen right now, she'd be at the stove, apron tied, humming an old hymn, the scent of biscuits and chicory coffee wrapping around her like a shawl. She wouldn't ask what had happened. Not yet. She'd wait until the room felt safe enough for the truth to land without splintering.

She wouldn't tell me I was strong. She'd remind me I'd always been.

The spell broke with a shift of light across the water. I pulled myself back, as if surfacing after a long dive, and the present returned—grass, wind, the grit of shore under my palms. After a while, I stood and dusted off my jeans. I walked the shoreline a little longer, picking up a smooth stone here and there, rubbing it between my palms as if it might hold answers. Then, I returned to the car.

The leather seat warmed under me. The scent of tobacco lingered. I closed my eyes and imagined my father beside me, quiet as ever, hands folded, waiting. He wouldn't have known what to say. But he would have shown up. He always did. That mattered more than I'd ever understood.

I drove back slower, letting the wind rush through the open windows and the sun kiss my shoulders. I didn't know what awaited me at Gran's. I knew only something had shifted.

I had gotten out of bed.

I had left the house.

I had driven my father's car down roads that still remembered me.

And I had not disappeared.

That would have to be enough for now.

CHAPTER 4:

THE DRIVE

BONES BENEATH THE PRAIRIE
Roseann Mayer

I turned onto the highway and rolled through town, past storefronts that hadn't changed in twenty years. Gran's quiet pressed in at my back, and I hadn't figured out where I was going. I needed only to move.

The Cadillac hummed under me, Daddy's car: big, blue, smooth, with power steering light enough to skim with a fingertip. I checked the rearview, met tired, alert eyes, then looked away and gripped the wheel a little tighter.

The sun was low; the shadows long. Sprinklers woke in front yards, crepe myrtles bowed, mailboxes crooked. A screen door slammed somewhere behind me. I didn't wave. I didn't stop. I just drove.

I drove the way you do when you're trying not to wake up ghosts. Beyond the gas station, I remembered a Friday night in a pickup, belts of wind through an open window. The church where I sang carols in a white robe, halo of pipe cleaners and tinsel. The downtown drugstore, first lipstick—slick, too red, Mom insisting I blot it till it looked natural.

The town seemed smaller—streets narrower, trees thinner—but the light was the same: clean, honest Texas light, illuminating all the parts I hadn't planned on facing.

I circled back toward my childhood neighborhood on purpose.

Oakmont Street hit me like a stone. Our old house, pale and small at the base of One-Mile Hill, looked exactly as I remembered. The carport leaned; the pecan tree stretched a crooked limb over the drive, as if willing hello. The storm door stood sentinel at the front.

My earliest memory came wrapped in sunlight, dust, and North Central Texas summers. I'm about three, my little sister wobbling beside me. We stand at the storm door in white cotton panties, eyelet lace at the legs making us look like Southern belles in training. Buck naked otherwise, for backyard adventuring.

That storm door was the gateway to the carport—the front line of defense. Mom whispered, as if not to wake a snake, "Check the step!" We'd peer down at the concrete and out across the shade, miniature soldiers surveying enemy territory—because rattlesnakes loved warm concrete and shade.

They paid taxes on danger; I suppose. Our house sat at the base of One-Mile Hill; Daddy trenched under the fence and lined it with screen wire to keep them out.

We learned early: always watch where you put your feet.

Most houses were the same: mid-century, with wide lawns, carports mingled with clapboard and asbestos siding, two or three bedrooms, one bath, humble, affordable.

Miss Thelma's kitchen was small—two steps from sink to stove, worn linoleum. It glowed anyway. Morning sun filtered through lace, turning everything into a soft halo. Cookies cooling on the counter, a pitcher of Kool-Aid guarding the fridge, smiling as if he knew secrets.

Bette and Sandy were sisters in all the ways Louise and I couldn't manage. Miss Thelma was everything. Hair set like a page from *Good Housekeeping*, lipstick for breakfast, apron tied just so.

We sat cross-legged on the floor, four girls in cotton shorts and bare feet, Kool-Aid in hand. The window fan rattled. Miss Thelma hummed a hymn. The world outside—daddies who drank, moms who worried, houses with sharp edges—faded away.

Christmastime brought a silver tree that spun in the living room, lights shifting through red, blue, green, gold. I'd lie on the floor, hypnotized by the glow. Magic. Pure, humming, colored-light magic.

The backyard was our kingdom: playing doctor under the willow, daring each other to peek into the Bishop's goldfish pond, scooters on the sidewalk until breathless. Our playhouse—the crown jewel of childhood—was a dingy 1940s drilling-rig doghouse Melvin hauled over and converted.

❧ INTERLUDE—THE PLAYHOUSE

At the far edge of Miss Thelma's backyard stood the playhouse, our crown jewel. Four little girls carved out a world of our own between the clothesline and the chain-link fence, where the dirt alley began. There was nothing grand about the structure—just wood, mismatched nails, and the smell of dust and laundry soap—but inside, we could stage every kind of a child's imagination could conjure.

Bette, Sandy, Louise, and I rotated roles with the solemnity of seasoned actors, but I always knew where I belonged. If there were a crown to wear, I claimed it. If there were a throne to fashion from an orange crate and a red wagon, I sat tall upon it. They indulged me, my loyal constituents, pulling me in procession beneath the flapping sheets on the clothesline, the pressed jeans pinned neatly on their metal frames like banners marking the edge of my realm.

My mother's discarded cocktail dresses became gowns. A tarnished tiara from a long-forgotten New Year's Eve party sparkled on my head as if it were genuine. Old high heels slipped from my feet as I walked the dirt path, sunglasses turning me into someone older, untouchable, already a queen. For a scepter, I decorated a stick with foil scraps and buttons, anything that caught the light.

When two of the girls yoked themselves as a team of horses, pulling me through the back gate and onto the alley, I reigned over more than a backyard. I presided over kingdoms of dust and light, a sovereign surveying her domain. The rattle of wagon wheels, the laughter of my companions, the hot West Texas air rising in waves—this was, yes, but it was also truth. For those hours, I was not pretending. I was ruling.

What I loved most was not the pageantry but the power of imagining myself beyond the confines of that little house or even my name. In my queendom, I didn't need permission. I didn't need to be quiet or small. I could declare myself radiant, worthy, chosen. My subjects—three giggling girls in worn shorts and bare feet—were not mocking me. They believed me into being.

Looking back, I see how much I lived in that role, how my imagination was not just play but practice. I was learning to inhabit stories, to test the boundaries of identity, to speak as if my voice carried. I was rehearsing for a life where words, not crowns, would become my inheritance.

And it matters to say this: in that backyard, in that playhouse, I knew exactly who I was. A girl unafraid of her own crown, sure of her place in the world she made. Later, that knowing would be stripped away—lost to silence, to fear, to years of believing other voices over my own. But for a brief and shining season, I carried it effortlessly. I was a queen, and I knew it.

That kingdom is gone now, but its echo lingered as I turned down Oakmont Street, where memory's bones still crunched beneath the gravel.

৯৶

Oakmont's gravel crunched memory's bones, and I saw it still there—the old sputter rig, rusted and overgrown with Johnson grass, yet standing. Daddy had brought me there once, at six years old, saddle shoes and pigtails, explaining what every pipe and pulley did. His calm, patient voice—different from the stormy man at night.

The rig looked tired, but the bones were there. Just like mine.

I didn't cry. I didn't need to.

I'd come back to remember. To reclaim.

For a moment, I let the girl I was rise—the sunburned shoulders, the head full of dreams, the loud laughter, the wide, bright world she carried.

I needed to hold on to her now.

Chapter 5:

The Sputter Rig

◆◈◆

Bones Beneath the Prairie
Roseann Mayer

Back in the car, the road stretched out in front of me—hot, cracked, and humming with cicadas. I rolled the window down, letting the dry wind carry off the fragments of memory that still clung after the playhouse. Not a victim. Not a ghost. A survivor. A soul reclaimed. A voice rising—strong, steady, full of grace.

I stepped back into the world outside, memory in dust and rust, in the heat that presses back. Close to where I grew up, the old sputter rig stood off the road—a relic no one could bear to tear down—leaning, sun-faded, intact. I hadn't planned to stop, but the sight pulled me in—one detour among many on this long drive full of revisited memories.

I parked on the shoulder and stepped out, the roadside grit whispering beneath my flats. A warm breeze stirred the dust as I crossed to stand before it. Paint worn to gray, metal arms rusted in place—bones of a giant buried beneath memory. It smelled of grease, sun, and old stories.

This rig wasn't sacred or famous—just an old workhorse from the 1940s, retired to a small park near Oakmont Street where I used to ride. Daddy and JC Jones had christened it, and it had sputtered and groaned, turning hard land into fortune and easing fear's grip.

The rig's silence now felt louder than its rattle ever had. Once it had been the pulse of our town, pumping possibility into every kitchen table conversation. Men measured their worth in hours spent beneath rigs like this. Women measured theirs in how well they kept beans simmering and children fed while the rigs demanded their husbands' backs.

JC Jones wove our lives together. Not a presence to admire, but a foundation you could lean on.

Silver curls, a crooked grin, an Open Road Stetson. A perpetual cigar clamped in his teeth. He forgave the mischief you were about to cause and made you want to try again. He taught me to bait a hook, drive a tractor, stand tall when the world tried to shrink you. He'd hold the door for a lady, tip his hat in church, then curse a spark plug on Sunday afternoon. Somehow, it all made sense.

I remember him guiding a combine through wheat, me on his knee like a cowgirl-in-training, the fields rolling out in golden waves. Later, at Albany Lake, he helped me laugh through the shock of a dunk in cold water. He smoothed things over for my mother as if it were nothing more than a sneeze.

He carried kindness like some men carry knives—always at hand, never needing to be sharpened.

I remembered a summer when I rode between JC and Don Baird in a tired '37 truck—no seatbelts, no radio—just wind and the hum of tires on caliche. JC struck a wooden match against his boot. "Light it?"

He handed me the map of West Texas from the glove box, saying, "Every road's got a story. Some just take longer to tell."

The map stayed in my lap; the smoke curling into the leather, the moment rooting itself in me as proof that trust could burn and light the way.

For years I've thought of naming a son after him.

When the well dried up during the drought, he showed up with a new tank and elbow grease, setting things right with a quiet insistence that didn't need thanks.

When someone in my family got sick, JC brought fans, a cooler, and a watermelon from the icehouse. He sat with Daddy on the porch after dusk, trading stories while cicadas buzzed. And when things got hard, he hugged me and told me to breathe, to move.

"You get on out of here awhile, baby girl," he'd say, and I'd hear a dare to survive.

The oil crash slowed everything, and he still came back with a story, a gift, a reminder that the world could be larger than fear if you kept your boots laced and your heart open.

When I left for college, he handed me *The Old Man and the Sea*, his name inked inside the cover. "You'll understand it someday," he said. I didn't then. I do now.

The sputter rig hadn't run in decades, but its rattle lived in my memory—the same beat that had once pulsed through this county before the world crowded memory out with progress.

I circled the frame, fingertips tracing the rusted edge. A dove rose from the scrub, wings slicing the quiet. I laughed at my jumpiness and told myself to stay.

I remembered the summer I came home from college, stranded outside the lake turnoff with a flat tire. JC pulled up, assessed the scene, and said, "There ain't nothing here that can't be solved with a little elbow grease and a cooler head."

He handed me the jack. We worked side by side, sweat and grit, and he handed me a red shop rag and a Coke. "You're stronger than you think," he said. "Most folks are. They just forget."

I forgot a lot after that, or buried it deep. But the rig dragged it all out again.

Back at the car, I lingered one last moment, the metal warm beneath my palm. A train whistle moaned somewhere in the distance, the sound of leaving something behind.

I sank into the seat, the horizon a question mark at the edge of the shimmer ahead. I didn't know where I was headed, but I knew I was moving.

I could carry him—the memory of JC, the rig, the stubborn land— into the next mile, and that would have to be enough for now.

CHAPTER 6:

THE LION AT THE BRIDGE TABLE

BONES BENEATH THE PRAIRIE
Roseann Mayer

I didn't swing straight back to my grandmother's house. The Cadillac breathed out heat and memory as I followed Albany's edge where country begins, letting the road pull me toward a place I'd long tied to my own pulse. Air, solitude, a landscape that knew my name even when I pretended it didn't—that was the work I came here to do.

The highway narrowed and then narrowed again, each mile a hinge in a door I kept trying to close on the past but couldn't quite shut. Caliche ground under the tires sounded like a stubborn grain that refused to be forgotten, and the land stretched in long, softened breaths.

The cattle guard appeared—our old gate to the Ibex Ranch—rattle and all. I slowed, listening to the undercarriage's percussion, a familiar rhythm that stepped into the cabin with me.

Albany's edge gave way to the Ibex Ranch's memory-threads. The road in wore the language of a country novel, curling toward a scene I'd thought I'd left behind.

The house rose into view like a green-walled dream, time wearing the wallpaper's wrinkles and the porch swing's creak like a language older than the words around it. The barn tilted a little, red fading to the color of memory's teeth, and peacocks wandered the yard as if the property itself owned the light. Birds cried in a chorus fit for a procession; chickens skittered away, as if the world itself remembered our footsteps.

But there, at the center of memory, stood the lion.

Not a symbol or a dream, but a real creature who had once slid beneath a bridge table during card nights, and with the audacity of a thing that has learned the geometry of rooms, rose mid-hand to disrupt the order of the game.

Lion wasn't a pet, and he never simply amused. He was Boone's daring proof that danger and charm could share a living room.

The cub's fur held a sunlit dusk, the warmth of a summer's edge. He planted his velvet paws on a buffet and—one of those stubborn truths that stories insisted on—knocked every bowl and platter in one sweeping arc, then retreated beneath the bridge table with a muffled purr as Aunt Mary Katherine swiped at him with a dishrag like a mother shooing a storm from the kitchen.

Lion belonged to them as surely as their shadows did, and the room never feared him for longer than a heartbeat.

Aunt Mary Katherine stood at the stove, skillet in one hand, a joke on her lips. The world might rage beyond the porch, but in her kitchen, time slowed to a simmer. She moved with the practiced tenderness that turns life into a letter you open with friends who arrive without invitations but belong anyway.

Her bracelets clinked when she moved, and her voice—half honey, half steel—could hush a room or lift it into laughter. She smelled of lavender and rain, and when she hugged you, the embrace pressed courage into your chest and whispered that you were meant for more than you'd become.

Lion wasn't a threat to me. He wasn't a dare. He was a question—an invitation to measure where fear ends and wonder begins. A creature who asks you to see wildness not as chaos but as kinship: a reminder that the animal inside you still share ground with the animal in the cage, the field, the house, and the heart.

Albany is a town of quiet embers and sudden storms, of driveways that end at a kitchen door and begin at memory's threshold. In those rooms—the kitchen's steak aroma, the clock's conspiratorial patience—I understood I wasn't just returning to belonging. I was returning to a version of myself that remembers how to stand on the line between danger and grace and not blink.

When I finally stepped outside, dusk wore the land like a crown. The baby would wake soon, and my grandmother's table would bloom with cloth napkins, heavy silver, and roast beef resting like a small sunrise.

The lion's presence, in memory or in the room, offered a moral: wildness belongs if you give it a place inside the ordinary.

I lingered a breath longer, letting the lion settle into the room's corners as a gentle invitation rather than a show of force.

The Cadillac rumbled on, and the late morning sun stretched into a patient, forgiving shape. I drove toward my grandmother's light, toward tea and roast beef and the steady, stubborn truth that memory, like the land, will always pull you back to what you need most: belonging, courage, and the quiet power to let wildness belong to you.

Chapter 7:

The Wedding

Bones Beneath the Prairie
Roseann Mayer

The drive back from the Ibex Ranch was quiet enough to hear the clockwork of memory turning in my chest. The lion still walked beneath the bridge-table of my mind, a soft, ancient reminder that wonder and chaos can share a room if you keep the door open and the floor clear.

Albany's edge gave way to Gran's house, where roast beef and sweet tea waited like old friends. The water tower rose in the distance, a sentinel of promises kept and promises broken, and I felt the pull of the wedding I carried with me—a memory dressed in satin and fear, a girl who once believed in fairytales and found herself pregnant with a different future.

Lunch was quiet, a ritual of breathing in and out without fanfare. My mother cleared plates with the grace of someone performing a hard spell, while Gran folded linen with a tenderness that made time feel almost edible. The baby's high chair stood empty, crumbs of cornbread clinging to its tray like small witnesses.

While the baby slept in the front room, I lay on Gran's twin bed, the silk bedspread catching the light as if it were listening. The noonday sun pressed through the blinds in a version of patience I could almost swallow.

I showered slowly, the water never hot enough—a small ritual to remind me that comfort, like love, isn't always instant. The ache in my belly and the ache in my heart spoke in the same language, and I listened, not with fear but with a quiet courage I hadn't known I had.

Gran tapped on the door and handed me a small bag—hairbrush, a blush, a pair of heels that might still fit. "Just enough to get you through," she said, her eyes holding a map of the years we'd walked together.

She kissed the baby, a soft weight against her chest, and then sent me toward the dawn of the wedding.

The hallway was hushed, every surface polished and ready, as if the house itself was determined to hold the day together. My dress waited in its tissue, pale yellow and generous, a cousin's gift that refused to shrink. It fit in the way memory fits a story you tell yourself over and over until it becomes true.

When I stepped into the hall, the world sharpened: my mother, coiffed and flawless, my father in a charcoal suit, both a sculpture of expectations. Yet, even in their composure, I caught the smallest betrayals—her hand tightening on her purse strap, his jaw working as if to hold a thought back. They were trying, in their own brittle ways, to steady me.

Gran stood by the door, with the baby in her arms, her eyes soft with unspoken things.

The car hummed toward town, Albany's square receding as if it knew a chapter was about to begin. Through the window, mesquites bent in the wind, their shadows stretching like questions across the road. My father cleared his throat once, then said nothing more. My mother applied lipstick from a silver tube, her compact mirror catching a flash of my reflection. For a heartbeat, I saw myself the way she must have: a girl already branded with consequence, yet expected to smile anyway.

The wedding house—a grand two-story limestone crown with green awnings fluttering like whispers—held its own breath of ceremony.

We moved through the kitchen, past the servers who worked with clockwork precision, past gleaming silver and the hush of a room primed for a moment larger than life and smaller than fear.

Aunt Evelyn appeared, elegance personified, a conductor keeping time with a smile. She swept in, perfume lingering like punctuation, and touched my arm with a warmth that both steadied and unsettled.

Uncle Clifford lingered at the edge of the crowd, broad-shouldered and shy, a quiet witness to belonging.

Then I saw it—the cake. Ida Mae Stark's genius in six tiers, a monument to craft and memory. Frosting roses spiraled like scripture, each petal coaxed into permanence. I remembered my own, built by her same hands, a sugar cathedral at the Petroleum Club.

For decades I kept its delicate topper, cherubs and blossoms frozen in sugar, until one move too many shattered it in my hands. Even now, I could see it—how fragile hope can be, how easily beauty crumbles.

Victoria, the bride, moved through the room in a column of ivory silk. She looked like a movie star, not only because she was stunning but because she had rehearsed this moment her whole life. She kissed my cheek and whispered, "I'm glad you're here."

Her words steadied what was about to break.

The clink of glass on crystal summoned us to the wide terrace. The sun began its slow descent, gilding the limestone as guests drifted outside in linen and seersucker. My mother sparkled under the pergola, surrounded by old friends, while my father stood darkly handsome with silver sideburns, smiling and mingling as expected—an actor in a role he knew by heart.

I held a ginger ale, smiling on cue, but my heartbeat pressed like a drum I hadn't learned to quiet.

My sister Louise drifted past in garnet silk, practiced coolness in every step. She gave me a nod, nothing more—no greeting, no sister-hood. She didn't ask about the baby. She didn't pretend to understand. But I knew she saw something and kept it locked inside, a quiet blaze stored for another day.

In Albany, people know what they know even when they don't speak it aloud—the rift between sisters, the bruises no one names, the prayers that never leave the room.

When the last cork popped and the peonies wilted, I slipped back to Gran's rambling single-story.

In the front bedroom, the baby slept curled against the quilt, one arm over his bear. My belly pressed steadily beneath the borrowed dress, another quiet reminder.

Moonlight silvered the mesquite outside the window. I unzipped the dress, letting the fabric fall around me, and pressed a palm to my belly. The room hushed, two hearts beating, both stubborn, both need-ing to be carried forward.

If a house could cradle a creature that defied the rules, then perhaps my heart could cradle a life that defied the odds.

Somehow, despite everything, I believed both hearts would be enough to carry me forward. And in that quiet, under Albany's mes-quite moon, I understood: weddings were not only ceremonies of love but declarations of survival. A vow to keep moving, to keep growing, to stay brave enough to let wonder stay.

❧ INTERLUDE—THE GOOD YEARS

There was a time, brief and blurry, when things seemed almost good. Not perfect, but enough to pass for love if I squinted.

We lived in a small brick apartment—one bedroom, the kind of place memory insists was warmer than it really was. The carpet was thin, the windows drafty, but in photographs it looks bathed in golden light, as if nostalgia insists on tinting the truth.

On Sundays he scrambled eggs and left the comics folded at my plate. There were kisses in the produce aisle, slow dances in the kitchen with a baby balanced on my hip. I kept a notebook of milestones on the counter. "First tooth," "first haircut," "first song hummed almost in tune." I thought if I wrote them down fast enough, the cracks in our lives might not widen.

Some afternoons we drove to the lake, hot wind tangling my hair while he told stories about fish that got away. We ate fried chicken from a paper box, laughter spilling out like it belonged to us. At night he lay on the floor with the baby, turning socks into animals, and for a moment I believed tenderness might last.

But the cracks showed. His corrections in public. The silences that followed questions. And in private, the slaps when I confronted him about the women who never really left—his ex-wife, the mistress who hovered at the edges.

His moods filled the room like a storm, and I learned to step softly, to walk on cracked glass and call it home.

Still, I strung pearls of happiness where I found them—marigolds in the garden, flea-market Saturdays, flowers in a mason jar on the table. I knotted them together and prayed the necklace would hold. But the clasp was always loose. Slowly, the milestone book gathered dust, casseroles gave way to wrappers, the marigolds shriveled in their beds.

Even in what I called the good years, I felt like a guest in my own life. I was playing wife, playing mother, hoping the roles might become true. What I clung to was not peace but the hope of peace.

If there were good years, they were stitched from fragments—moments bright enough to endure the rest. They glitter in memory like pearls, but pearls can break. One sharp tug, and the string scatters across the floor, rolling into corners where I can't reach them again.

And it was out of those broken years—out of the thin ground I tried to stand on—that the summer nights grew heavy. The Texas air hung thick with heat and cicadas, the kind of night that pressed against the windows until it felt like the walls might give way.

By then, the necklace was already scattered, and I was living on borrowed light.

Which is why, when the phone rang in the dark that night, his voice on the other end carried more than a threat. It carried the truth I had tried for years not to see. Reality.

CHAPTER 8:

HOT SUMMER NIGHTS
AND THE NEXT DAY

BONES BENEATH THE PRAIRIE
ROSEANN MAYER

The cicadas don't stop. A ragged choir rising from the dirt, humming through the heat. July holds its breath, heavy with creosote and dust. My bare feet press the porch boards still warm from the sun. They creak, each groan carrying into the night like a signal that someone is awake who shouldn't be.

The light above buzzes, moths throwing themselves against it like they'll never learn. Their wings make frantic, papery sounds, a soft thrum against glass that reminds me of fingernails on a screen door. Somewhere down the block, a door slams. A dog barks, short and sharp, then quits. And then nothing. Just the night, holding me in its fist.

The air tastes like mesquite smoke carried from someone's pit down the street, mixing with the metallic tang of heat-baked dust. I breathe through my mouth, shallow, as though the night itself might burn if I inhale too deeply.

Tomorrow will bring the parade—the horses, the off-beat band, the old fire truck polished to a dull shine. Once, I loved it. Peppermint sticks raining down, my mother laughing when I caught one, her clap like I'd won a prize. Lemonade, sun, music. A sweetness that belonged to another life. Now, the same sounds feel like a snare waiting to spring.

Main Street already looks haunted, chairs lined up like a welcome for ghosts. Canvas lawn chairs faded from years of use, some tagged with masking tape names to hold spots, others standing like sentries no one had called for. Ghosts of cousins and classmates, Sunday school teachers who'd once pressed peppermints into my hand after hymns. Tomorrow they'll line the curbs, all eyes pretending not to stare, not to whisper.

For tonight, I am staying here. Lock the door. Check the latch. Again. The baby's bottle, measured, tested. Again. Lying down, sheet tucked up, heart pounding like a drum, I can't still.

And then the phone tears open the dark.

Not a ring—an alarm. My father's borrowed flip phone shakes once, then screams. The sound slices through the stillness so sharply it feels like glass cracking. My body moves before thought does—I snatch it up, press it hard to silence the second ring. My hand shakes, sweat slicking the keys.

It's him.

"You have my son," he says. Voice low, sharp as a blade. Each syllable is a cut, the kind that doesn't bleed right away but burns slow.

"You think your daddy can protect you? Think anyone in that little town will stop me?"

A pause. The kind where breath freezes.

"I'm already here."

Click. Silence.

The words hang in the dark long after the line dies. I don't wake my parents. My breath stops in my throat, caught like prey waiting for the rustle in the grass. Sweat slides cold down my back, soaking the sheet. My heart thunders, each beat a warning drum I can't quiet. Because he's done it before.

Memory slips in, sharp and small: Carrie was my island. With her I let down slivers of myself, just enough to breathe. But even her yard wasn't private for long — once or twice I'd catch him in the alley, a quick flash at the window that turned a polite laugh or a cup of coffee into something brittle. I was never alone long enough to relax; he kept me off balance, afraid to speak because of what might come. Shame wrapped around me for having let it happen and stayed. The smell of Carrie's apple cobbler drifts up in the recollection — meant to mean safety, but in me it curdled, mingling with the old terror. He wanted me to know he was there. Always there.

Sometimes I'd slide into my car and find his cologne on the passenger seat, a jacket planted like a calling card — his way of saying he could reach me anywhere. I believed him.

Now, in Gran's house, I grip the curtains and watch the yard. The gate latch swings once; a shadow shifts across the grass. My throat closes. Just a moth. Just the night. I press myself back against the wall as if plaster could keep him out.

My baby stirs in the Pack 'n Play, a soft whimper, fists curling tight in a dream. His skin smells faintly of powder and milk. I hover, watching his chest rise, rise again. Proof that he's here, that I've kept him safe—at least tonight.

I don't wake my parents. I know what happens if I do—sirens; the sheriff showing up with his pistol in a boot, his promise of protection too loud, too theatrical. And then all of it turned back on me. Every word twisted until I'm the one with the explaining to do. Better to stay still. Better to bear it alone.

I cradle the swell of my belly, hand spread over taut skin. The baby kicks, small but defiant, as if to answer: I'm here. I'm coming. I am not afraid of him.

Tears sting, but I blink them back. Not here. Not now. Fear is a luxury. Survival is the only rhythm left.

The night crawls on. Shadows lengthen, stretch, dissolve. I pace the floor in silence, checking the latch again, whispering lullabies into the humid dark. The cicada's drone, a low chorus threading through every thought.

At dawn, the mockingbirds take their shift, calling across the trees, bold and bright. The sky bleeds pale pink over the rooftops. The night folds back into memory—the porch light, the moths, the phone burning in my hand.

I am worn down, shaking, hollow-eyed. But not finished. Not yet.

The morning quiet stretches thin. I know it won't hold. It never does. Fear always cracks through.

Today, I will walk into the parade, shoulders tight, eyes forward, scanning every shadow. I will pretend the freedom I'm fighting for is already mine. Pretend long enough to make it through the route.

I've learned better than to trust a bright summer day.

If I can survive the one more day without breaking, maybe I can survive the parade too.

One mile at a time.

Chapter 9:

The Fandangle Parade

—◈—

Bones Beneath the Prairie
Roseann Mayer

Morning light slid across the red clay like spilled milk—soft, almost harmless. But the light couldn't mask the day's tension, or the air that seemed to hold its breath. It crept through the blinds, pooled on the floorboards, lit the dust in the corners, and nudged the baby to stir. A dog barked in the distance. A screen door slammed. Farther off, a rooster crowed again, though the sun was up.

I sat up slowly, legs heavy with dread. The baby had stirred before I did, cooing at the ceiling fan. I dressed as if it were just another Saturday. No drama. No ceremony. Just motion.

Then the ritual: we loaded into Daddy's Cadillac. I was in the backseat, with the baby on my lap. The stroller wedged in the trunk like a suitcase we'd forgotten to unpack. Mother sat up front, fanning herself with the folded program from the Fandangle rehearsal, lipstick already perfect. Daddy tapped the steering wheel like a metronome, eyes squinting against the bright sun. It felt almost ordinary—like every other Fandangle parade day we'd known. The kind of day where tradition wore dust and pretended everything was normal, even when it wasn't.

I tucked my fear beneath the wipes and burp cloths, beside a half-crushed snack pouch and a broken rattle. Then, carefully, with practiced ease, I lifted the baby into the stroller as if he were spun glass and wheeled him onto the street.

The parade crowd was already waking the town. Flags snapped in the breeze. A trumpet blared a shaky version of "The Eyes of Texas," rising and falling like a half-remembered prayer. Grease and cotton candy mingled in the air. Teenagers sipped Big Red from Styrofoam cups. Babies squirmed under lace bonnets. Grandpas adjusted lawn chairs. The town shimmered like a postcard left too long in the sun. A child cried, then squealed. The sound rose and fell like a bird skimming rooftops.

Of all the ways I imagined returning, none involved standing on Main and Jacobs with my heart in my throat, watching my sister glide past like royalty. Side-saddle, draped in gold, the crowd applauded as if she hadn't exiled me from her world long ago.

Louise moved like a woman claimed by the crowd—rapt in admiration I could no longer access, elevated by something I once understood but no longer owned. Louise wore gold velvet. Black velvet trim hugged her bodice. A gleaming gold top hat perched on her head, its veil shimmering in the sun like a banner announcing triumph. She rode her golden dun with a spine so straight and her head so still you could balance a book on it.

She waved, that slow, deliberate smile perfected for the moment of applause. She was a vision. A warning. A memory on horseback.

And I stood there in the dust, alone with a baby in a stroller, trying to pretend I didn't feel the sting rising behind my eyes. I held my breath, clinging to composure as if it might keep me from unraveling. Don't cry, I told myself. Not here. Not in front of them. If I cried now, the whole town would see. And she'd win again. My hands gripped the stroller until the pulse throbbed in my fingertips. The crowd clapped and waved, blissfully unaware of the battlefield inside me.

What I saw wasn't just my sister. It was everything I'd lost. Everything I used to be. The space between us—a canyon I'd never cross—felt that day wider than ever.

Louise hadn't been beautiful in the same way I was. That's not vanity—that's how the world sees us. I was the spark. She was a stone.

Even as girls, we knew our roles. I played to the room. She pulled back. They crowned me homecoming queen. She passed me the tiara as if it burned her hand.

Now there she was—gold-draped, side-saddled, praised. A high priestess in velvet. Untouchable.

The baby squealed with delight. I forced a smile for him, nodded to neighbors, and pasted on a grin as if nothing had happened. My lips cracked at the corners from the effort.

But I kept glancing over my shoulder. Because I knew what he was capable of. And I knew he wanted me afraid. I kept moving. I kept searching for my daddy in the crowd, behind the shaded alleys—just in case.

My ex was a coward, and I knew he'd never act where someone might see. I felt safer in the crowd, but fear still pricked the back of my neck. I didn't dare leave Main Street's safety.

My feet moved along the route memory had drawn for me, even as my mind split: one half bracing for danger, the other seeking comfort in the past. Pushing the stroller past familiar shops and facades, nodding to familiar faces while my stomach churned with the possibility that he could be crouched behind any parked car or shade.

Every slow-moving truck made me flinch. A loose muffler clanged, and I jumped. Every man in sunglasses and a ball cap looked like him—for a half-second too long. My pulse thundered in my ears, drowning out the music and cheers. I knew better, but fear makes fools of the sharpest women. The baby's toy skittered to the sidewalk, and I crouched to pick it up, eyes never leaving the crowd.

I moved on, up Main Street, toward the places that had framed my life: the old drugstore with penny tiles spelling CARTER'S Rexall in faded green, black, and white; Idol Ages, my grandmother's shop, still whispering royalty with its clean hangers and lavender starch; the hotel that wasn't a hotel anymore, now a park, but still a ghost at the edge of memory. I pictured my mother and grandmother stuffing mailers for the Chamber of Commerce, the oak table, the dry tongues after licking envelopes.

Creosote, lemonade, hot dogs on the grill—memories braided through the air. A girl could almost believe she was still that version of herself, untouched by betrayal, wrapped in a thrilling illusion that nothing truly bad could happen here.

Every step pulled another memory forward—chalk dust, the clack of dominoes on Miss Thelma's kitchen table, cicadas screaming in the heat, the hem of an old dress brushing past me.

I thought of Daddy lifting me onto his shoulders so I could see the floats, the smell of Aqua Velva and coffee. Back then, I believed he could carry me through anything. Nothing in this town could hurt me if I stayed close to the ones who knew me best.

And yet—

The weight on my chest wouldn't lift. Because I wasn't a child anymore. I was a mother.

Now I walked the same streets with fear knotted beneath my ribs, not sure if the devil I'd run from was behind me or ahead.

My son gurgled in the stroller, one sock kicked off, his toes pink in the sun. I smiled at him, waved to Mrs. Neff, adjusted the satin ribbon in my hair, and tucked the blanket around his legs like armor.

And I kept moving.

Toward the courthouse. Toward the gazebo. Toward the brick and dust that built me.

I wasn't sure if I was walking toward something or away from it.

But the road was unfolding. And I was still on it.

Later, when the last float had passed and the brass notes faded into the air, I found my parents waiting near the car. Daddy's hat tipped against the sun, Mother's lipstick still perfect, both of them standing like sentinels by the Cadillac. I pushed the stroller toward them, my son babbling, his cheeks flushed with the thrill of the balloon man in his hand.

We didn't speak of fear or shadows. We just gathered ourselves back together, as families do, and walked to the car. My son had seen his first Fandangle parade—cotton candy, flags, applause—and he had loved it.

For that moment, at least, joy belonged to him. And that was enough.

CHAPTER 10:

RAISED BY FIRE AND FROST

❖

BONES BENEATH THE PRAIRIE
Roseann Mayer

Teenagers peeled off in cliques toward the Dairy Queen. Mothers folded lawn chairs and gathered diaper bags.

My son dozed in the back seat, mouth slack with sleep and sugar. His tiny fingers still curled around a balloon string—long deflated, but clinging weakly to memory.

I was back in the car with my parents—Daddy steady at the wheel, Mom poised beside him. With the baby asleep behind me, my breath grew shallow, chest tight. It felt like slipping back into a childhood photograph. Silence filled every crack between us. Not peaceful, but practiced. The kind that knew its place. I was ten again—not speaking. Not asking. Just going along, because that's what kept the peace.

Yet, unease prickled under my skin as I watched cotton-colored clouds drift by. I was a mother now, carrying a voice and a child and a truth inside me. But in this car, I felt myself shrinking—unsure if I could bring all of who I'd become into the space I once called home.

"Let's drive out to the cemetery," Mom said, rummaging in her purse for sunglasses, as if the thought had just struck her.

Daddy nodded, turning the wheel on instinct. "The flowers looked rough last time. We need to check."

I wanted to speak. To puncture the quiet. But the words tangled and fell flat, and the silence stretched.

It was tradition—every Fandangle weekend, wedding, family gathering—we ended up at the cemetery. Not about grief, but presentation. Order. Grass trimmed just so. Vases upright. Mom marched along the gravel path in kitten heels, purse tucked under her arm, critiquing arrangements like ribbons at a county fair.

Daddy walked slower, quieter, as if the dead might still listen. He straightened a flag, brushed leaves from a stone, but rarely spoke sentiment aloud. Still, I felt it. I'd spent years aching for his attention, learning to read it in gestures, not words.

I longed for him—the safe lap, the silent shadow who brought order when everything else felt wild. I never doubted he loved me. He just never said it out loud.

The past felt like a room I was trying to enter, but the door was half-closed. I wasn't sure if I was welcome anymore.

We walked like this, the three of us, as always. Mom led with purpose. Daddy followed quietly. I trailed behind—part daughter, part ghost. Not invisible, but hollow. The space between us thickened like glass. I could see and hear, but couldn't reach them. The hum of the Cadillac, the tick of the turn signal, my own soft breath—everything felt distant. Present but unanchored. Holding a secret so heavy, I thought I might float away if I didn't keep my hands pressed to my lap.

I leaned my head against the window, glass hot against my temple. Each thrum of the tires drummed through my bones. The heat grounded me, but my thoughts wandered—to what I'd lost, what I'd buried, and the question pulsing behind my eyes: when did I stop feeling at home in my family?

I wanted to go back—to the girl who laughed without fear. But I knew that girl was gone.

We passed the elementary school without a word.

It hit me like a jolt. Low and sprawling, sun-bleached, weathered by decades of West Texas wind. Dusty pecan trees still shaded the time-weathered swing set. The flagpole leaned, rust blooming like a bruise. The cracked sidewalk yawned wide, as if the earth itself had tried to split open.

That schoolyard had raised me in ways my parents never could. There, I learned to read silence, navigate injustice, and find my name in a crowd that never called it.

At school, they might have punished my voice, but someone heard it. At home, it only echoed down hallways like a sound no one had time to answer.

I spent more time cross-legged by that flagpole than on the swings. I couldn't stop talking—God help me, I came by it honestly—and Mrs. Speck gave up, making me the school's first-grade scarecrow. Silent. Sentenced. Watching recess unfold like a show I wasn't invited to join.

I learned early that words carried weight—sometimes too much to bear.

In third grade, I told a girl she was pregnant because she'd grown breasts. I didn't mean it cruelly. It was like announcing a weather change, unaware of the weight my words carried. She ran crying. They sent me to the nurse's office for "moral correction."

That moment carved something inside me. My first taste of shame wrapped in curiosity—the beginning of learning that truth, especially from a girl's mouth, often came with consequences.

Her pain became the echo chamber where my voice learned to hesitate. A recoil that shadowed me for years. That hesitation seeped into my bones, shaping how I spoke to friends, bosses, lovers. I scanned the room before speaking, anticipating disappointment like weather. I held my truth until it lost its urgency.

I didn't know then, but that moment by the flagpole became a map of my emotional cartography—each pause, each silence, a path retraced.

But when they called Mom ...

She came in like thunder in heels. Lipstick perfect. Hair shellacked into a helmet. Pearls resting just so. I was still on the little cot when she grabbed my arm and launched.

"You do not say things like that; do you hear me?"

She spanked me. In public. In front of the secretary, the janitor, everyone.

Then the nurse—God bless her forever—stood in the doorway, arms folded, and said, "Virginia, you were ten times worse. Leave that child alone."

Mom froze. A flicker crossed her face—shock, defiance, maybe both. Then she sniffed, waved it away like smoke, and marched me to the car as if nothing had happened.

That was Mom—a wildfire in red lipstick. Bold. Exacting. Impossible.

Everyone said I was just like her. God help me, I was.

I was burning my way—waiting to see what would catch fire.

Therapy taught me it wasn't rebellion. It was an inheritance. A legacy passed not by word, but by fire.

Where Mom funneled hers into control—committees, casseroles, call sheets—I struck matches and waited to see what would burn.

Once, at eight, I lit a kitchen towel on fire just to see if anyone would notice. The lemon oil made the flames leap like dancers—beautiful and terrifying, sacred and forbidden. I screamed when the smoke hit the ceiling. Neighbors came. So did the fire department. I buried my face in a dish towel while shame wrapped me like smoke.

I never admitted it. Not then. But I did it. I wanted to be seen. Not just noticed, but truly seen—the way Mom lit up a room and Daddy disappeared into one.

I wasn't trying to mimic her or rebel against him. I was trying to break the silence. To feel the heat of attention, even if it came in smoke and sirens.

Daddy was quiet. Measured. Brilliant in his way. He loved order—crossword puzzles, quiet mornings, the *Wall Street Journal* folded crisp. He loved Mom, but she wore him down, one blaze at a time.

He came from East Coast blood—a Wellesley-educated mother, older sisters white-glove clad, prim, proper, speaking in code and expectation. Boarding schools, engineering degrees, pocket squares, restraint. Not grief exactly, but practiced detachment. It made it hard to know what he felt, even when he was right beside you. He managed emotions instead of expressing them. Folded neatly. Packed away like pressed shirts. Handled, never spoken.

Between fire and frost, both shaped me—or tried to.

As we rolled past the schoolyard, the silence inside the Cadillac felt like a presence.

Mom had once stood there, on that dusty yard's front lines, demanding something this town wasn't ready to give. She ran for school board when women weren't supposed to. She won election. In office, she voted to integrate schools when it still meant not everyone would agree, there might be consequences.

It was the early sixties. People called late at night. Daddy unplugged the phone more than once.

He didn't want her to run. Not because he disagreed, but because he knew the cost—the threats, the stares, the way our house trembled like a matchbox in the wind. She came alive in conflict. He wanted peace.

They loved each other. But love isn't always a sanctuary.

By the time she lost re-election, integration had already moved forward. But something inside our home fractured. They never spoke of it. They drifted. He tinkered in the garage. She baked casseroles she never ate. The silence grew so wide I could live inside it.

Now, decades later, I sat in the back seat—seven months pregnant, silent, sweating. Praying no one would ask the wrong question. Wondering if I'd make it through the weekend without cracking open like glass.

I was folding in on myself, shrinking into the upholstery. The Cadillac didn't feel like a car. It felt like a waiting room between two lives—the one I'd already left, and the one I hadn't named yet.

I pressed my thighs together, hands flat on my lap, willing myself not to dissolve. Wondering when I'd stopped being her daughter and started being her echo—just another soft footfall behind her, repeating steps I no longer believed.

But something in me had cracked.

And once the remembering started, I wasn't sure I could stop.

The road ahead shimmered like a mirage. Something split open inside me. No turning back.

I didn't know where I was going yet—but for the first time in a long while, I knew I wasn't going back.

❧ Interlude—What I Thought I Deserved

I didn't marry a man who adored me. I married a man who saw me as a possession—an object to be owned, not a person to be loved. From the start, tenderness was absent. In its place came rules, silence, and power dressed as passion. I was told you earned love through obedience, endurance, and extinguishing your own needs.

And I—young, desperate to be chosen—wrapped those conditions around my heart like a veil. I called it commitment. I called it marriage. But it wasn't. It was captivity. And I walked in willingly.

I married a man who wanted me possessively, cruelly, destructively. He consumed me like something to be claimed and conquered. There were no gentle moments between us. No slow dances in the kitchen. No apologies. No warmth when the world grew cold. I became someone to manage, correct, and diminish whenever I dared to want more.

Despite that, I clung. I went after him like a drowning girl clutching a stone, calling it rescue. I chased him. I convinced him. I told myself the ring would fix it. That a wedding was a doorway to belonging. That being married meant I was wanted—and that being wanted was enough. I told myself it was love, because I didn't yet understand what love wasn't.

He didn't love me. He told me as much. Sometimes with words. Mostly with silence. Despite that, I stayed. Why? Because somewhere deep in my bones, I believed I didn't deserve better. I believed love was a transaction: effort in, scraps out. That love required sacrifice, submission, and a willingness to disappear just enough to make room for someone else's rage.

I wanted to be touched without shame. I wanted to leave my parents' house with my head held high and a white dress to prove I was worthy. I mistook the relief of being chosen for love. I thought if I could be wanted, I would finally be safe. But what I truly wanted—even if I couldn't name it then—was something gentler. A love that didn't demand performance. A steady, honest love. One that didn't require me to shrink to fit inside someone else's idea of who I should be. A love that didn't come at the cost of my voice, my light, my spark.

Instead, I chose someone who mirrored the silence I'd grown up inside. Someone who punished what was bright. Who saw need as weakness. Who made longing feel like shame. And I let him for years. When you are raised in measured quiet and conditional approval, you believe that love must be earned in silence. That longing is something to apologize for. Being chosen matters more than being cherished.

I stayed. Not because I was weak, but because I believed that if I could just be better—quieter, thinner, more agreeable—he would soften. That he would finally learn how to love me. He never did.

The hardest part to admit? I lit that match, too. I walked into that house. I said yes. I packed my bags and crossed a threshold I didn't yet understand. I stayed through the first slammed door. The first shattered glass. The first apology that wasn't really an apology. And with every compromise, every silent morning, every step away from myself—I became someone I didn't recognize. I buried the girl who once filled rooms with laughter. I muted the part of me that dreamed out loud.

And when it finally ended—when silence turned to shouting, and shouting turned to fear—I blamed myself. Because if you grow up believing love is something you earn, you will always think the loss of it is your fault. It took years to unlearn that lie. Years to understand that love isn't supposed to make you small. That it doesn't ask you to bleed. That genuine love—healthy love—holds you as you are. Unconditionally. Without cruelty. Without silence as punishment.

I wish I could go back and hold the girl I was. The one who wore white lace like armor and called it devotion. The one who believed that survival was love. I wish I could whisper in her ear: You are already enough. You don't have to trade your fire to belong.

But I can't go back. All I can do is write it down. Name it. Hold it to the light.

And with that promise, I stepped into the quiet that follows reckoning—the stillness before a new beginning.

The driving faded behind us. But I carried the truth with me now—named, spoken, unburied. The road ahead waited, and I knew I wouldn't go back. I stepped into the next chapter with a breath I'd earned—and with the memory of the bones I refused to leave buried.

The veil had lifted long enough for me to see what had stood between me and myself. Now the veil would be ripped wide, and I would walk into the world—not as what I survived, but as what I became.

Chapter 11:

The Veil Ripped

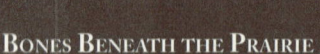

Bones Beneath the Prairie
Roseann Mayer

The spell of memory broke as the car doors shut. We left the cemetery in silence. My mom adjusted the air vents with the precision of a woman arranging place cards at a funeral—controlled, deliberate. My dad checked the rearview mirror and steered us back toward town with the same focus he once used on oil rig schematics. No one mentioned the parade. No one asked if I was okay.

Main Street looked like a stage struck clean. Confetti clung to curbs; boot prints pressed into the dust. A soda can rolled across the sidewalk, and a hand-lettered sign lay crumpled beneath a lamppost. The air carried a faint, stale scent of popcorn and smoke.

The limestone courthouse, proud since 1883, stood sentinel at the center of town. The jail squatted behind it, order and consequence side by side. Bluebonnets pushed through the uncut lawn, stubborn against the heat. And above it all, the clock tower rose like a watchman, marking time, bearing witness.

We crossed the Clear Fork Bridge—the same one where, as a child, I had tossed wildflowers and watched them swirl downstream like nameless prayers. The Beehive Saloon stood shuttered in the sun. The old

sputter rig came into view, skeletal and stubborn, planted beside the feed
store like a rusted weathervane measuring memory instead of wind.

We passed my childhood neighborhood and descended the quiet
slope that led to Gran's house.

Her low-slung stone ranch glowed beneath the porch lights, flower-
beds clipped neat as fingernails. Cicadas shrieked into the dusk. Inside,
everything gleamed: drapes drawn taut, waxed floors reflecting golden
light, the air still and expectant. Gran hummed in the kitchen, laying
out cold cuts and casseroles as if it were any other Saturday.

Dinner unfolded in a hush—the clink of silverware, tea in sweating
glasses, the quiet pulse of the fan. My dad offered me potato salad. My
mom adjusted her necklace, her voice bubbling with pleasure as she
named off the people she'd spotted in the parade—one of those rare
moments when she let control slip and happiness spill out unchecked.

I half-listened, watching my son curl on the velvet couch beside the
poodles, fingers sticky with syrup.

By ten the house was still. Gran helped me nestle the baby to sleep
in the front bedroom, left a nightlight glowing in the hallway, and told
me to holler if I needed anything.

Then, my cell phone rang.

It lit up on the nightstand like a warning flare. My thumb hovered.
It was him.

His voice coiled through the speaker—low, breathless, familiar in
the worst way.

"They served me with your divorce papers. You think you can hide?
You think your family can protect you?"

"Stop calling me," I whispered.

He laughed, sharp as glass. "You don't get to tell me what to do. I
told you I was there last night—you just didn't see me. Doesn't matter.
You'll see me soon enough, and nothing's going to stop it."

Click.

The air thickened.

I had heard that voice in stairwells and parking lots. In dreams. In silence. Once, a single red rose wilted on my windshield—a threat dressed as romance. He left notes without names. Called and breathed, then hung up. Voicemails filled with silence. A shadow lingering too long at a window. A reflection that didn't belong.

He unraveled my reality until I questioned every creak and flicker. I whispered in my house. Slept in jeans with a flashlight under my pillow.

When I finally spoke—to pastors, friends, a counselor—he framed it as instability. Calm. Measured. A masterclass in control. Once, he planted sunglasses in my glove compartment and accused me of infidelity. He would tilt his head and say, "You always imagine the worst." And for a while, I believed him.

But it wasn't imagination. It was survival.

I slid off the bed, back against the wall, breath ragged. Something brushed the window—a rustle. The drapes no longer softened the room; they turned to shadows.

Barefoot, I crept down the hallway, fingertips trailing the cool plaster. My parents were just steps away, but it felt like miles.

My dad was already awake, perched on the bed in striped pajamas. "What is it?"

I told him everything: the call, the threat, the sound outside. And what I had just learned—it was he who filed the divorce papers. Not me. Not yet. I had wanted to, but fear and confusion kept my hand still, and in the silence my father acted first.

"I did what I thought was right," he breathed. "We couldn't wait any longer."

I nodded. Not in agreement, but because there was no time left to argue.

He rose, pulling on his burgundy robe. My mom stood in the hallway, phone to her ear, alerting family and allies. Her face was pale; her voice was steel. No one said, danger. No one said, divorce. But we were leaving at dawn.

Sleep was impossible. I sat in the window seat, counting lightning strikes, listening for the clock's half-past chime.

Gran came in, robe wrapped tight, carrying warm milk. She didn't ask questions. She sat beside me, hand resting on my shoulder, and hummed "Rock of Ages." Her presence was prayer. Her silence, shelter.

At first light, I dressed the baby, wrapped him close, and left a note on the counter beside her cinnamon candies: *I'll call when I can. Love you.* My dad packed the car with tight efficiency, as if folding fear between the suitcases. My mom made sandwiches with trembling hands but wore her pearls anyway. Gran stood on the porch as we pulled away, one hand lifted in goodbye. I held my breath until the house disappeared.

CHAPTER 12:

THE ONE-MILE HILL

BONES BENEATH THE PRAIRIE
Roseann Mayer

Part I: The Leaving

O nce again I was leaving a place I loved and longed for in my dreams. The rain had let up, but the road ahead shimmered like a slick ribbon beneath a low sky. My father drove in silence, hands firm on the wheel, eyes fixed just past the curve—as if staring too closely at the present might undo him. My mother sat beside him, composed, her body angled slightly away, lips pressed tight. The quiet between them was old and familiar—like wallpaper you no longer noticed.

In the back seat, I kept my eyes on the road behind us. Watching for headlights. For him. I imagined him circling already—too late, too soon. The baby finally drifted to sleep, warm and heavy in the crook of my arm. I moved my other hand instinctively to the round of my belly. She stirred there—my daughter—not yet born but fully present. A flutter beneath my ribs, like a moth caught behind lace. I pressed my palm against the movement, as if to whisper: *I feel you. I'm still here. We're still here.*

I let myself believe—for a single, stolen mile—that we were safe.

It was a long way from Albany to West Texas. And it would be an even longer journey back. One I wouldn't make again for decades.

But I had done this drive once before. I was fourteen, curled in the back of our station wagon, my face smashed against a suitcase, watching Albany disappear. My grandmother had stood in the driveway waving until we turned the corner. No drama. No protest. Just that quiet, stubborn strength she carried in her bones. The press of her palm against mine. The Mason jar of iced tea she packed for my mother. The folded twenty she slipped into my hand felt like a secret.

I never told her I didn't want to go. Back then, we didn't say what we needed. We just went along.

Now, I sat in the backseat of another car—older, exhausted, swollen with child—and still not entirely sure how I got here. A duffel bag at my feet. A half-packed diaper bag. My baby beside me, and another just beneath my skin. I was leaving again. Only this time, I wasn't chasing anything. I was running.

The landscape outside was as familiar as breath—mesquites bending low, fences sagging, pump jacks nodding like they knew something I didn't. The road stretched long and quiet, dappled with puddles. A hawk cut across the sky. A buzzard circled.

The silence in the car wasn't peaceful. It was practiced. My parents had lived inside it for years.

"Did you bring the maps?" my mother asked, breaking the hush like a dropped plate.

"They're in the glove compartment," my father answered, eyes never leaving the road.

That was it. That was all.

I closed my eyes and let the hum of the tires carry me back: to Gran's kitchen, the lemon scent of dish soap, the peach ice cream melting too fast on summer porches, the hymnals too heavy for my lap. I had thought I would forget it all. But I hadn't. Those memories returned like postcards slipped under the door—bits of who I had been.

It wasn't just a town we were leaving. It was a version of ourselves.

The baby stirred in his sleep. I tucked the blanket higher, thumb tracing his cheek. His face carried the promise of the sister he didn't yet know—the same almond-shaped eyes, the same stubborn chin I would come to recognize in her. The same soft weight of history pressing forward in flesh and breath.

I thought of her too. Not yet born, but already carrying the echoes of every choice I had made. Her kicks had rhythm now—a drum, a whisper, a prayer.

Someday, I would tell them the truth—what we left, why we ran. *This is what silence costs.* But not yet.

The one-mile hill came into view. Albany behind us. The road curving forward. My chest tightened.

I didn't turn back. I whispered, "Goodbye." And we crested the hill.

If you've ever left home—truly left, with hands trembling and heart breaking—you've sat beside me on this road. If you've ever held a child close while your past reached for your throat, then you've known this silence. This courage. We don't always get to choose what breaks us. But sometimes, we get to choose what comes next.

… This was the choice. Mine. Thank you for riding it with me.

Part II: The Road

The tires hummed their steady hymn, the rain softening to mist. My forehead rested against the glass, and for a heartbeat, time collapsed—the road ahead, the road behind, both pressing in at once.

And for just a moment—I wasn't thirty-one, pregnant, and running. I was fourteen. Summer of 1969. In the back of our Mercury station wagon, pressed between a suitcase and a crate of dishes, sobbing as the town disappeared. I'll never forget that road; its mesquites and fences imprinted on me, the red clay fading into the horizon ...

Daddy had taken a promotion with a West Texas oil firm. A larger salary. A new title. A big adventure.

My mother called it opportunity. She told herself it was for us—for new schools, new friends, new horizons. She even wore high heels for the drive, her pearls fastened too tight. I watched her adjust them when she thought no one was looking, her fingers lingering just a moment too long at her throat.

I was chubby, loud, the girl who didn't get invited to pair up at slumber parties. The girl who wore the wrong shoes, said the wrong thing, wanted too much. Albany was beautiful. And it was suffocating. They feared I'd never escape it. Louise was blooming then, arms crossed in the middle seat, refusing to say goodbye. She had the most to lose. I wanted to reach across my heartbreak and comfort her. But I couldn't.

The car smelled of dogs and Juicy Fruit. Daddy's ice chest kept sliding across the vinyl floor. The cascading light struck the dashboard and turned the dust to gold.

I held the last flyer from the Fandangle in my lap; the ink smudged with tears. My finger traced the covered wagon on the page. I pressed hard enough to leave an imprint.

That hill—this hill—marked the end of something. Albany didn't just disappear behind us. It lodged inside me like a splinter. The place I tried to outrun, then spent my life trying to return to.

At seventy, it's Albany that sings to me. Cicadas, gospel harmonies, the heat rising from stone. The songs I once sang without shame. Nostalgia isn't weakness. It's a prayer. A map back to a self we didn't know we were losing.

And now, here I was again. Another backseat. Another goodbye. Only this time, I wasn't chasing anything.

I was surviving.

The light shifted—clear, slanted, holy. The grasses flickered like fire. My sweet baby stirred. I pressed my hand to my belly.

"We're going to be okay."

Leaving is never clean. The dust clings. The ache roots deep in your bones.

But this time, I wasn't leaving a town.

I was leaving the man who hunted me. The silence caged me. The life that had been swallowing me whole.

And that, I learned, was the hardest road of all.

❧ Interlude—The Kingdom of Flame

The old drilling rig doghouse was a sight: a rusted spaceship with oil-stained walls and pinup posters clinging to plywood. It looked as if it had fallen from the sky. Melvin, our neighbor two doors down, hauled it in on a flatbed and parked it behind Bette and Sandy's house as if he knew children needed kingdoms. Not castles with moats, but places patched with grease and grit. Maybe he remembered what it felt like to want a world of his own. Or maybe he just saw us, barefoot and half-wild, and thought: they need something sacred.

We were five, maybe six—the sweet-spot years when imagination blooms unbothered by self-consciousness. Our voices rang across the yards like bells; knees scabbed; hands sticky with summer. Louise was there too—just outside the center. She played, but I rarely imagined her as central. I was the one with the vision. The leader. The queen, if anyone asked. And sometimes they did.

The grown-ups scrubbed the rig shell clean. We dragged in orange crates for chairs, pinned sheets for curtains, laid down baby blankets for rugs. We called it a playhouse, but it wasn't. It was a palace. A church. A stage. Some days it hosted garden parties; on others, funerals for dolls wrapped in towels, wailing over them like saints. It was glorious. It was ours.

We had rules: you had to knock; you had to be sworn in. There were titles, ranks, trials by feather. Our names shifted—Lady Firebrand of the Hills, Sister Magnolia of the Southern Order—crowns cut from Reynolds Wrap, scepters made from broomsticks. In that crooked space, we ruled like giants.

And somewhere in that tangle of sheets and orange crates, I fell in love with fire.

Not destruction, not danger. But fire as presence. The hush of a match catching, the flicker of candlelight painting stories on plywood walls. I stole taper candles from my mother's drawer and stashed them beneath the crates. We lit birthday candles in jelly jars and called it ambiance. With candy cigarettes and Kool-Aid in teacups, we imagined ourselves women with secrets, free of curfews and consequences.

We whispered real things too—confessions and questions we didn't yet know how to name. And when they felt too heavy, we buried them in jars beneath the dirt, waiting for time or someone wiser to understand.

Until I got caught.

A single match, still warm in my fingers.

My mother's face blazed into the doorway like a storm, fury and fear braided together. She yanked me out by the wrist and sentenced me to exile. No playhouse. No kingdom. No stories. I was seven.

The girls carried on without me. From behind the chain-link fence, I built a lean-to from blankets, crowned myself with twigs, and made banquets from mud pies. Louise passed me notes through the wire, little decrees that reminded me who belonged inside and who didn't. It wasn't cruel. It was the law.

That was when the fire moved inside me.

I missed the ritual—the shimmer of candlelight, the way our world glowed when lit from within. I missed being the one who named the games. Who started the story. Who led.

One afternoon, alone in the kitchen, I struck a match again. It caught the corner of a lemon-oil rag, flared, and died. Enough to scorch the silence. Enough to remind me I wasn't powerless.

Her scream when she smelled the smoke is one I still carry—not because she was cruel, but because she was afraid. She loved me. She didn't know what to do with a girl who loved fire.

That small blaze earned me parole. When I returned, Bette and Sandy welcomed me back as if a queen was restored. Even Louise, solemn and proud, stepped aside to give me my seat. No one asked where I had been. They poured Kool-Aid, passed pretend pie, and the kingdom rose again, whole in an instant.

I cried that day—not for the fire, but for the ache of exile. For the sting of lost power. For learning too young that what you build can be taken. And for realizing I was strong enough to build again.

Years later, I lived in grander houses, with sweeping views and polished counters. But nothing matched that crooked playhouse: the hum of candlelight, the daring in dirt, the clang of a broomstick scepter. It was the first place I learned to rule. And the first place I learned what it meant to lose my crown.

The fire stayed. Not rebellion. Not ruin. But presence.

§

Even now, when I strike a match to light a candle, the flame leans toward me—as if remembering. And I bow my head toward it, remembering too.

Even now, when I strike a match to light a candle, the flame leans toward me—as if remembering. And I bow my head toward it, remembering too.

The years carried me far from that castle of plywood we called our playhouse—and still do—into houses with vaulted ceilings and clipped hedges, where lemon polish erased every trace of dust. Yet the ember from that kingdom never left me. I carried it like a hidden jewel, a reminder of the crown I once wore so easily, before I knew how fragile crowns could be.

In those polished rooms, the air cooler, the corners staged to perfection, I moved carefully, as if a queen in exile. Still, the fire bent toward me, whispering of a reign once claimed, a crown once lost, and the light that refused to be extinguished. And always, beyond the shine, there waited a hallway—its silence stretched tight, its final door closed against me.

CHAPTER 13:

THE DOOR AT THE END OF THE HALL

◆—◇◈◇—◆

BONES BENEATH THE PRAIRIE
ROSEANN MAYER

The house smelled like her: Tea Rose perfume, lemon polish, and that faint trace of luxury that could feel cool at first but softened if you stayed long enough. A 3,300-square-foot traditional—the last house built in one of West Texas's coveted neighborhoods. Corner lot. Boxwoods clipped like hedges at Augusta. Old money. Oil money.

It was a house meant to be admired. And lived in like a performance.

The parquet floors gleamed like a stage. Silk drapes pooled in perfect folds. A chandelier from New Orleans hung above a table for twelve, rarely lit, never touched. A towering cabinet displayed Steuben, Baccarat, and Haviland, silver trays and crystal goblets—every piece a sermon on order and legacy. Though my parents didn't drink, we sipped sparkling cider at Christmas, pretending not to notice.

Off the kitchen, the butler's pantry led to a maid's dressing room and bath—unused, waiting for a ghost. Our housekeeper even ironed the sheets weekly. Under my mother's reign, no wrinkle dared remain.

And now I was back.

Not as a daughter. Not as a guest.

As a shadow.

They placed me in what had been Louise's room. Now it was mine—sort of. Same green carpet. Same twin bed with its stiff brocade spread. Only now, an antique iron baby bed stood in the corner. My mother had flown it home from Denver on a Learjet, determined her grandchildren would sleep in it. It passed no safety codes, but it was staying. It was a lovely piece of furniture.

Slouched at the foot of the bed was a diaper bag. Dread pressed on my chest like a second pregnancy.

I didn't unpack.

My son, flushed from heat and fatigue, slept. I sat on the edge of the bed, hands folded like a child awaiting reprimand. The hum of central air whispered through the vents. A strip of hallway light glowed beneath the door. I left it open a crack—I needed to hear everything. Every creak, every voice, every car slowing too long outside.

This house wasn't safe. But it was where I had been told to go. Like a safe deposit box—enclosed, protected from weather, but never from the storm inside.

My parents believed in protocol. In distance. They thought his threats were bluster, that the restraining order was armor.

But I knew better.

I could still hear him—boots pounding the stairs, his breath close on the phone, the way his hand once slammed against the wall beside my head. He had charm like a switchblade. A grin that could draw blood. And I knew no locked door—not even the one at the end of the hall—would stop him if he came.

Even if he never showed, the damage was done. The fear lived inside me now, carried in my ribs like breath. Fear builds its architecture slowly, and it doesn't collapse just because someone hands you a key.

The room was orderly, softened by framed prints and muted light, but the stillness pressed in. I lay back, eyes tracing the ceiling, willing my thoughts to settle.

In another life, I would have called Louise. But she and I had been estranged since childhood. Once, when I tripped in the schoolyard and skinned my knees raw, she walked past me without a word, while others knelt to help. That silence stretched between us for decades. Even at seventy, I still don't know why she despised me. Maybe resentment. Maybe fear. She never told me, never gave me the chance to repair it. When she died, the distance ended without either of us mending it.

And even if she had answered, I wouldn't have known what to say.

Fear gripped me. Anger too. I thought about walking down the hallway to my parents' room, asking if I could climb into their bed like a little girl. But I was too old. Too ashamed. So I stayed awake, wrapped in layers I couldn't shed.

That night, I slept in my clothes.

I woke before dawn. The birds had begun their rehearsal, though the sky was still blue-black. I peeled myself from the bed, careful not to wake the baby, and padded to the kitchen.

It was spotless, of course—every surface gleaming. My mother had set the stage the night before: filters stacked, cream waiting in its cut-glass pitcher, cups aligned like soldiers. The air smelled faintly of lemon and starch.

I found the silver canister where it always was. Measured beans. Water. Button. The percolator hissed and gurgled, a sound so familiar it felt like muscle memory. Like a hymn I no longer sang but still knew.

Steam rose in spirals. I cradled the cup in both hands, letting the heat settle into me. Outside, the clipped hedges glistened in the first light. Stone paths curved to the corner where the Scotties patrolled—black, busy, unchanged. Orderly. Familiar. A picture of peace, though I knew peace and beauty weren't the same.

When my mother appeared—robe belted, hair immaculate—she didn't say good morning. She sat across from me, folded her hands, and spoke in that measured tone reserved for delicate matters.

"You can stay as long as you need," she said. "But we need to have a plan."

A plan. As if safety could be bullet-pointed.

My voice broke its silence. "And what if the plan doesn't stop him?"

She didn't answer. She just reached for her planner and wrote, her script neat and steady.

Later that day, my father and I walked with the baby through the neighborhood. Heat bleached everything into brilliance. The stroller wheels clicked against the sidewalk. My father's khakis were pressed sharply, his shirt tucked with care.

We didn't speak of the morning or my mother's plan, but I carried it with me—uncertain if it protected or contained me. My father didn't ask questions. He never did.

When the baby fussed, he offered his pinky. "You did the right thing, no matter what happens."

I nodded, eyes burning.

That night, I locked the bedroom door. Not because it would stop him, but because it was something I could do. The baby slept in the crib beside me, his small hand curling around my finger.

Still, sleep didn't come. The house held its breath. Past midnight, I rose and walked barefoot down the hallway—past the crystal cabinet and unopened mail—until I stood at the closed door at the end. My parents' room. The place where the lights never went out, where everything was polished and stored, where ghosts were kept behind glass.

For a moment, my hand rested on the brass knob. I thought about waking them. About showing them the shape of the storm inside me. In telling them the truth, I couldn't fit into a plan.

But I turned away.

Back in my room, I sat on the bed and watched my son's chest rise and fall. His breath warm, his hand gripping mine in sleep. The quiet pressed in, heavy and unbroken.

And finally—finally—I let myself weep.

CHAPTER 14:

THE LIE I LIVED IN

BONES BENEATH THE PRAIRIE
Roseann Mayer

But weeping brought no rest.

I didn't really sleep—not the kind that heals you. I drifted in fits, jolted awake by phantom sounds: the groan of floorboards, the hiss of pipes, the Scottie dog Maggie's nails ticking in the dark. The baby stirred once, and I pressed my palm to his chest, waiting for the rise and fall. My blue-eyed boy. The only light in a world that shifted like sand under my feet.

My parents knew only a fraction of what I was living through— one-tenth, maybe. I never told them the rest. If they had known, they would have been horrified. They might have locked me away, or even tried to take my children, out of fear for their safety. And maybe they would have been right to. But they didn't ignore me. They simply didn't know. Because I never let them.

But it wasn't him I feared.

It was quiet. The kind that lets memory slip in and rearrange the furniture.

He had that salesman's sheen—quick with a smile, quicker with a pitch. People humored him, sometimes even liked him, but beneath it all was the sense he was always angling for something.

In the quiet, I saw him again. The man I married. Not handsome, but dangerous in his stillness. Dirty Clint Eastwood, I used to think—weathered skin, crooked teeth, a carpenter's apron slung across his chest like armor. His shop was a squat, windowless box at the edge of town, the air thick with varnish and sweat. He didn't smile. Didn't flirt. Just stared, as if he were memorizing me.

He didn't charm me. He curated me.

And I let him.

I knew what he was capable of. Years earlier, when I ran, he punished me. My car disappeared from my parents' driveway in the night. Two days later, he "found" it—gutted, seats slashed, dashboard torn apart, the stench of ruin clinging to the steel. It wasn't a car anymore. It was a warning.

Still, I went back. Pregnant and humiliated, walking across a college campus full of backpacks and bare legs, I let him find me. He showed up with God in one hand and forgiveness in the other, his voice soft enough to sound sincere. Counselors saw effort, not manipulation. My parents saw stubbornness, not survival.

And then—once—he kissed the crown of my head, gentle as a prayer. Just once. That single gesture was enough to keep me wondering if there might be more. That's how control works—it hooks you with scraps.

I walked a tightrope between two dangers: one wore control like propriety, the other like possession. I thought I could manage both. But I couldn't.

So, I swallowed the truth, blamed myself, and let the lie take root. If I were good enough, obedient enough, holy enough—maybe he'd love me the way I needed.

But deep down, I knew.

He didn't want love. He wanted control. And I wasn't ready to leave.

I stayed in the lie. Because leaving meant admitting everything I had built wasn't a house at all—it was scaffolding, fragile and temporary, rattling in the wind.

Even now, I wonder who would want to read this—who wants to sift through the ashes of someone else's fire?

But I keep going. Because if you're still in the smoke, I see you. You're not alone. Survival doesn't look tidy. Healing isn't clean. But it's possible.

CHAPTER 15:

THE RETURN

BONES BENEATH THE PRAIRIE
Roseann Mayer

One afternoon after classes at the community college, he found me in the parking lot. He was waiting by my car, leaning, casual, rehearsed—eyes soft, voice contrite. He begged me to come back. He said he couldn't live without me, that this time would be different, that we would go to Christian counseling together and learn to love each other the way God intended. He made it sound holy, inevitable. He knew the language that could still undo me.

I couldn't even hint to my parents that I was considering it. If I had, they would have locked the doors and never let me leave the house again. They knew what he was capable of. They feared what he might do if I went near him.

So, when they went grocery shopping that afternoon—the way they had for thirty-five years, slowly, deliberately, knowing the clerks by name—I knew it was my only window.

I gathered the few things I had carried into their house—my children, the stroller, a small bag of clothes—and tiptoed through the rooms. The air was thick with apple pie cooling on the rack and carnations fading in a vase on the kitchen table. Every sound was magnified:

the click of a latch, the scrape of a drawer, the squeak of stroller wheels on linoleum. An ordinary house, yet in that moment it felt like the walls themselves were listening.

At the side door, I hesitated, hand on the knob. The silence I was leaving would speak louder than any note. Then I stepped into the blinding Texas afternoon.

I didn't say goodbye.

I didn't leave a note.

I just vanished.

My mother had warned me through tears that she feared for my life. And still, I chose him—over her, over my father, over common sense.

They knew where I had gone.

What followed was silence. Not the hush of bedtime or the sweetness of a sleeping baby, but the kind that thickens with each day until it presses on your chest. My mother, who once couldn't go forty-eight hours without seeing the baby, disappeared from our lives. No cards. No calls. No coffee at her table. It was as if I had died, and she was rehearsing how to live with the absence.

That silence pulsed, a second heartbeat. It thudded in the background as I folded laundry, rocked the baby, washed dishes in a house that never felt like mine. The silence was punishment, but it was also grief—ours, tangled in ways none of us could name.

He tried to make things look decent. Mowed the grass. Hauled groceries. Talked about new plans. Once, he even brushed my hair back from my face and whispered, "We'll start over, you'll see." For a flicker, I almost believed him. But it was all for show. I was eight months pregnant, moving slower, carrying another child into a life already cracked down the middle.

By then, the oil had dried up, and West Texas itself felt brittle. U-Hauls rattled down Main Street like funeral cars, hauling away busted dreams. The sky went white with heat, dust curling behind cars bound for somewhere—anywhere—else.

He never paid the bills. One morning the faucet spat air, then nothing, until he scraped enough together to turn the water back on. I had no bank account, no keys, no say-so. Just a grocery allowance if I asked the right way.

Then came the knock on the door: eviction.

I stood in the kitchen, one child warm on my hip, the other asleep in a borrowed bassinet, staring at the paper taped to the frame. It was the blow you don't argue with—final, like a gavel. From there, the pieces fell, one by one: the house, the car, the furniture. I still remember standing barefoot on cold tile, watching two men carry off the last chairs. All of it bought on credit, all of it hauled back out.

When word reached my parents, he spun the story his way—said I'd spent too much, bought things we couldn't afford. Practical explanations for practical people. The truth was, I never had money of my own. My parents didn't give me any, and he only ever handed me grocery cash. If something was bought, it was because he said yes, not me. I might have asked for things, but I didn't swipe the card, didn't sign the check. I couldn't. That was his power, and he wielded it like proof against me.

My father didn't argue, but the space between us stretched like barbed wire across parched earth.

We filed for bankruptcy in the very town where I'd grown up, where folks still fanned themselves in Sunday school and leaned close to whisper. There was no hiding it. My name in black ink was proof enough.

We carried on. He drove us past shuttered houses and boarded-up gas stations, talking about new beginnings. I buckled the children into their seats, the belts hot from the sun, and tried to believe him.

But the prairie had already turned its back. And when the world looked away, I did the only thing I knew how to do—I turned inward.

The land that once held me in its wide embrace now felt like a witness against me, and there was no hiding from its silence. When the world looked away—neighbors, family, even the soil under my feet—I learned to look inward. Prayer became the only place left to stand. Not the kind recited in polished pews or whispered out of obligation, but the raw kind that rose when breath caught in your chest and you weren't sure you'd survive the night. That was my defense, my shield, my fire.

❧ Interlude—The Flutter of Fans, the Fire of Prayer

I learned early that prayer was my best defense—my sword against what pressed in on my life. Not just words strung together, but breath and fire. Prayer could be whispered, shouted, sung, or wept. When it was real, it carried weight. It moved. It shielded. And when silence from my parents pressed in, when eviction notices bloomed on doorframes, prayer was the only sound I had left.

But the 1960s CME Church in Albany—that was something else entirely.

The moment the doors opened, sound rose to meet you—low voices spilling over, laughter bubbling like a spring, the organ humming underneath. Stepping inside wasn't entering a sanctuary. It was walking straight into a heartbeat.

The air had its own liturgy: wax from polished pews, peppermint tucked into the purses of church mothers, a faint dust of powder pressed onto cheeks that day. Light streamed through tall windows, catching dust motes as if even they had been invited.

The women were radiant. Wide-brimmed hats tilted just so. Feathers trembling. Gloves smoothing hymnals. Scarves knotted bright and sure. And the fans—Lord, the fans! Paper-printed with scripture and funeral homes, snapping open, waving in rhythm, another instrument in the choir's hands.

Then the singing.

It never began with a conductor's cue. It started low. A hum. Then it caught fire. Sopranos soared. Tenors thundered. Tambourines cracked like lightning. Children clapped, feet stomped. The sound roared like a river: we are here; we are seen; we are heard.

Prayer there wasn't with folded hands and bowed heads. It was voices rising all at once, overlapping like waves. "Yes, Lord." "Mercy, Jesus." The "Amen" wasn't the end. It was the door flung wider, pulling in more sound, more hope, more fire. For the first time, I knew prayer could dance. It could shout. It could sing. For the first time, I felt it in my bones.

When my children prayed, it was different again. Their eyes squeezed shut, voices soft with trust, words tumbling out unpolished and sweet. No theology. No performance. Just love. Sometimes an amen ended in a giggle. Sometimes in a sigh. It always felt like music.

Prayer didn't live only in the sanctuary or by the bedside. It lingered in casseroles left on porches. In a napkin folded. The dish was returned with a note tucked inside. Sometimes prayer was silence itself—asking nothing, yet offering everything.

And when the house emptied, when the water taps ran dry, when silence from my parents felt like abandonment—prayer burned steady. It filled the hollow where words failed.

Prayer was the only thing that fed me when nothing else could.

Chapter 16:

The Unraveling

❖

Bones Beneath the Prairie
Roseann Mayer

The Houston metropolitan area held no promises for me—just more pavement, more noise, more places to hide.

We arrived like vagabonds: me, weary but still hoping; our three-year-old son; our baby daughter; and the man I had married, already sketching his next "big plan." Some scheme, he swore, would save us. Within a month of settling there, I was pregnant again. I remember thinking—if he could just hold a job, maybe we had a shot.

He never did.

We found a rental. Barely. The carpets smelled like sour rags; the linoleum peeled at the corners. But it had a roof. I took a job as outreach secretary at a small Baptist church, where I could smile and keep up appearances. The pastor called me a blessing. I typed bulletins that promised joy and peace, even as my hands trembled from the night before. I folded newsletters announcing revivals, potlucks, and fellowship hours, while I felt myself fading. The words were true for others; I only prayed no one read between my lines.

He was always chasing something. A supplement line. A mail-order "sure thing." A handshake in a hotel lobby that was supposed to make us millionaires. He came home with duffel bags of sample kits, spiral notebooks of scripts, but never with money. At first, I believed him. I joined him at kitchen-table meetings, invited friends, handed out brochures. Supporting his ventures felt like supporting my marriage.

Part of the trap was that, in the multi-level world, you couldn't just scrape by quietly—you had to look like you'd already arrived. The cars, the clothes, the dinners out—they weren't luxuries in that circle, they were bait. People had to see the "success" in order to want in. So, we lived beyond our means, not only because he was chasing the next big thing, but because the business itself demanded a performance of abundance.

But each scheme fizzled, and I grew weary of knocking on doors—literal and otherwise—asking people to buy into dreams that rarely paid the bills.

Ten months after we moved to Houston, our second son was born. No insurance. No cushion beneath us. Still, he came into the world like a flare over a flat, gray bayou—sudden, piercing, undeniable. His cry cut through the haze, his fists clenched with a strength that startled me. For a moment, the worry fell away. No unpaid bills, no cracked linoleum, no restless schemes. Only the warmth of new skin against mine, the miracle of breath and heartbeat wrapped in a hospital blanket.

He—my husband—lifted the baby once, and whispered, "He's strong. He'll make it." It was the closest he ever came to tenderness, and it nearly undid me. That scrap of softness was enough to keep me circling back.

My parents came. My mother gathered him as if she could fold his whole life against her chest. Silent tears streaked her face—tears for him, for me, for all that could not be spoken. My father sat near the window, still as ever. When I rose for coffee, I found a folded check slipped under my saucer. No words. Just a steady look—part pride, part sorrow—that said more than any speech.

They didn't stay long. Their visit was measured, as though obligation had carried them there, but something else lingered too. They had come for the baby, yes, but also for me, even if they couldn't name it. My mother called now and then. My father, without a word, sent money again when I admitted we were short on rent. The silence wasn't gone, but it had cracked enough to let in a sliver of light.

And as I held my son in those first days, his breath rising and falling against me, I remembered the girl I had once been—the lake girl with sunlit hair and open laughter. I could almost smell the damp wood of the dock, feel the wet sand between my toes. Looking at him, I felt her stir again, as if she had been waiting for this reminder: that life could still break through, even here.

We brought the baby home wrapped in a gift blanket, stocked with diapers from a church shower. The kindness of others covered the cracks, but only just.

He refused to look for steady work. Said he was too smart for hourly pay, too proud to take orders. I was "small-minded," he told me, for not believing in his dreams. Meanwhile, I was the one keeping the lights on, feeding the babies, driving five minutes to the church office each day—steadying myself in that quiet before his next plan swallowed us again.

I began to disappear.

Not all at once. Piece by piece. A smile here, a laugh there. The woman I used to be drifted to the far edge of the mirror. I wore hand-me-down maternity pants, scrubbed mildew from the sink while the baby banged a spoon on the floor beside me. I dried bottles and my tears with the same dish towel.

The shame never screamed. It whispered. It crept into corners, sat heavy at the breakfast table. It followed me into the night and woke with me in the morning, reminding me with a steady pulse: you chose this. And it was a shame I could not hand to my parents—it would have broken them. So, I held it close, silent, like a bruise beneath Sunday clothes.

By then, I had learned the shape of him. The small cruelties. The quiet power games. His strength depended on my bending low enough for him to tower above. Even his idea of safety was a trick. He hid money in coffee cans, glove boxes, under a broken lawn chair—calling it "security." I knew better. It wasn't protection. It was possession.

But life wasn't only shadows. Some afternoons, sunlight poured through the kitchen window and I watched the children chase each other in the yard, their laughter rising higher than the hum of traffic outside. For a moment, joy spilled into the room like grace, and I breathed easier.

At church, I found small circles of women who prayed over one another in whispers. With their hands warm on my shoulders, their laughter after the "amen" tugged a smile out of me when I hadn't felt one in days. I learned to edit my words, but their presence reminded me I was not entirely invisible.

Still, at home, survival diminished me. A pair of shoes for the children meant counting every penny. Groceries meant choosing what would last, not what I craved. I told myself if I loved harder, prayed longer, bent further, maybe the cracks would close. But deep down, I knew the walls were already shifting. The lie was still alive in me, and the unraveling had begun.

But even as I shrunk inside that Houston house, I could still feel her—the lake girl with sunlit hair and laughter at the water's edge—waiting to remind me who I had once been.

❧ Interlude—The Lake Girl

I could water ski by the time I was six years old.

On summer afternoons, my parents packed up the car, gathered my sister and me, and drove to Gene and Mary's place—a small stretch of private lake just big enough to feel like it belonged to us. The shoreline always looked like a painting when we arrived: towels draped over the car doors, coolers lugged down to the sand, the water shimmering like it had been waiting. Heat rose off the ground in visible waves, making the air ripple. Smoke from the grill curled upward, clinging to our clothes, while the sharp tang of Off! insect repellent hovered on our skin.

The lake had its own soundtrack: cicadas buzzing from the trees, the whir of boat motors echoing across the cove, laughter bouncing from one end of the water to the other. When we jumped in, the water carried its own smell—part fish, part gasoline, part mineral-rich earth stirred up from the bottom. It clung to our hair and skin even after a shower, a badge of where we'd been.

I was fearless then. Small but strong, my hands gripping the rope, my body trusting the pull. My father would crouch behind me, adjusting the skis beneath my feet, planting them just right. "Hold tight," he'd say, his voice steady, almost kind. My mother stood nearby in her sunglasses, a towel wrapped around her waist like a skirt, shading her eyes with one hand. The boat engine revved, the rope went taut, and then—sudden, violent motion. Spray stung my cheeks. For a heartbeat, I sank. And then, miracle: I rose. Wobbly at first, but then steady. Gliding.

Even though I was clumsy on land, always bumping into corners or tripping over shoelaces, something in me knew what to do on water. My arms burned, my legs trembled, but the rhythm carried me forward. The water didn't mock me or catch me off guard. It held me up when I leaned back and let go of fear.

Those lake days felt like another world. My sister and I ran barefoot through the sand, daring each other to jump from the dock, collecting bruises from scraped shins and not caring. My mother unpacked sandwiches from a cooler, white bread sticking to wax paper, potato chips crushed into curls at the bottom of the bag. She was different at the lake—looser, laughing, humming along to the transistor radio perched on a lawn chair. My dad laughed too, his shoulders softer, his face sunburned and unguarded. The weight he carried in town—at work, at home—lifted in the sun.

We didn't name it then, but those afternoons were their own kind of church. A sanctuary of water and light, where rules loosened and voices rose without hymnals. My father's laughter was its own music; my mother's wave from the shore its own benediction. Out there, we were still whole.

Later, we moved my grandfather's old office building to the lake and made it ours—a getaway patched together with hand-me-down lumber and dreams. The little house had no polish, but it didn't need any. The lake filled the cracks. And then came the sailboat. A massive flat-bottomed thing my father bought in Minnesota. It had to be shipped to Albany by railcar and offloaded onto a flatbed trailer. People came out just to watch, neighbors and strangers alike, curious to see how a boat too large for our small lake would be forced to fit. And he made it fit, like he always did. My father had a way of muscling the world into shape, even when it resisted him.

For me, though, it was always about the skis. The tug of the rope. The spray on my face. The way the shoreline blurred when the boat picked up speed and I cut across the wake. Leaning back and letting the water carry me felt like flying. Like freedom.

That girl on the skis—grinning, squinting into the sun, rope gripped in small hands—she still lives inside me. She was awkward and clumsy on land, but on water she was alive. Brave. Certain.

Sometimes now, standing barefoot on cracked linoleum in a Houston kitchen, a newborn pressed against my chest and bills stacked like tombstones on the counter, I remember her. The lake girl. Her laughter still echoes, faint but insistent, reminding me of who I was before silence and schemes pressed me small. She leans back inside me, trusting the pull, and whispers that I can rise too.

The lesson was simple but sound: when the rope tugs and the water pulls against you, lean back. Trust it. The same lesson that steadied me then steadies me now.

When I falter, she is there—the girl with sunlit hair and steady hands—urging me forward. She leans back, trusts the pull, and rises, showing me how to follow.

Chapter 17:

The Cabinet Shop

◆◈◆

Bones Beneath the Prairie
Roseann Mayer

It looked like a rescue. At least, that's how I wanted to believe it.

We were barely hanging on. Three babies under four. No money of my own. Lies and unpaid bills pressed so hard I could hardly breathe. My job at the Baptist church stretched just far enough for diapers, groceries, and gas—but never far enough to carry us. And he wasn't helping. Not really. He never had steady work, never brought home a paycheck. Always chasing the next great opportunity, always on the brink of a breakthrough that never came.

When the associate pastor at our church offered my husband a position at a small cabinet shop, it looked like a gift—quiet, honest work meant to tether him to something real. Something my daddy could believe in, maybe even wrap his calloused hands around as proof that his daughter was finally safe.

Daddy had spent his life running oilfield crews, balancing books, building things people could measure, fix, and respect. Dreams didn't draw him—order did. So when the offer grew into a chance for my husband to help buy out the business—eventually with the promise it would be gifted to me—Daddy urged us to say yes. To him, it looked like stability. To me, it felt like quicksand disguised as solid ground.

I only nodded, lips forming thanks while my heart clenched in fear. This wasn't relief. This was the ache of sinking lower, like a drowning woman handed a rope she already knew was frayed.

Daddy called it a legacy. A future. He told me one day it would be mine. But even then, I knew better: what looked like salvation could just as easily become another cage.

But it wasn't. Not really.

By then, I had left the church work behind and stepped into the shop myself.

The shop itself was a respectable business. Solid work, an excellent reputation, steady demand. I gave quotes, answered phones, made sales calls, and showed up at Chamber of Commerce luncheons to drum up new clients. I was the charm—the one in respectable clothes with the gift of gab and just enough education to win people over. He was the worker bee, keeping the books and delivering the orders. From the outside, it looked balanced, almost professional. But beneath that, the cracks were already spreading.

From the very beginning, my husband told me I wouldn't be paid until things "got going." We needed cash to build the account, he said. His paycheck, he promised, would cover our bills until the business was strong enough for mine to kick in.

But every month we came up short. Always another excuse: a client slow to pay, a client delaying pickup, a bank error he swore he'd clear. And I believed him. I stayed quiet, telling myself we were sacrificing for the future. I didn't tell Daddy—because I thought I was doing what a loyal wife should do, standing with my husband, trusting his word.

A year in, Daddy suspected. He showed up at the shop before lunch—no warning—sawdust dusting his boots like he'd walked through the workroom on purpose. He set his palm on the office ledger, looked at me first, then at him.

"Where are her checks?" Daddy asked, tapping the column where my name appeared beside half the invoices.

My ex smiled as if it was all a misunderstanding. "I figured since she's basically an owner, maybe you were paying her separately. I thought—"

Daddy cut him off. "Numbers don't think. They add." He slid the ledger toward me. "Have you been paid?"

Heat climbed up my neck. The truth sat heavy on my tongue. I wanted to believe my ex. I wanted Daddy to believe him too. But the blue lines on the page told a story my heart couldn't deny.

"No," I said finally, my voice smaller than I wanted.

Daddy's jaw tightened. "From this day forward, ten percent commission on every invoice with her name on it. Paid when the customer pays. Not someday. Not 'settled.' Paid." He didn't raise his voice; he didn't have to.

He pulled a yellow legal pad from his briefcase and slid it across the desk to me. "Write every job you bring in," he said. "Dates. Amounts. Keep your own list."

I tucked the pad in my purse that day, the pen writing in a steady, unforgiving blue. It wasn't much. But it was mine.

For a while, it worked. Daddy went through the books line by line each month himself. My commissions showed up like clockwork. From the outside, the numbers looked strong enough for us to build a two-story brick house in a nearby town. The plan was simple: household bills from my income, the mortgage from his. Daddy paid him a market-rate salary. On paper, it looked secure.

And in truth, he loved the work. He'd stay at the shop late into the night, sanding, measuring, checking deliveries. He came home smelling of sawdust and glue, his hands nicked with splinters, his shirt worn thin at the collar. For a while, I let myself believe the shop might be the making of him—that maybe he'd finally found something he could give himself to.

But then over coffee, he told me he was three months behind on the mortgage. Like it was nothing.

That's the news that shatters a woman.

When I asked how; why; all he said was, "You'll just have to go sell another job. Hustle something. Maybe we can catch up."

He liked to watch me squirm. Liked the panic in my eyes—it gave him power.

He never once said, "This is on me." Never once stood up as a man, a father, a provider. Instead, he lied to my daddy. Told him I was overspending. That I wasn't managing the budget. That I'd run us into the hole.

And Daddy—who had bailed me out more times than I cared to admit, who knew I'd never once balanced a checkbook—believed him enough to not ask questions. And why wouldn't he? I had a checkbook now, but only because Daddy insisted I be paid commissions. Beyond that, I wasn't managing a dime. I had no oversight, no access, no real say in how the money flowed. All I did was bring in the work. But when the blame landed on me, it sounded familiar enough to stick. That gutted me.

My parents called daily. My mom's questions came sharp through clenched teeth. Daddy's voice stayed quiet but firm: "What's going on down there?" "Why is he lying to us?" "Why are you letting him?"

Each time I opened my purse, touched the corner of that yellow legal pad, and felt the sickening truth: I had the records. I had the proof. Despite that, I stayed silent.

I found myself caught between two men: one who built me, and one who broke me. One who trusted me, and one who used that trust like currency.

And through it all, the house bore witness.

The walls heard me weep behind a locked bathroom door, my voice breaking in the quiet. The carpet held my pacing, the mirror, my hollow eyes. Even the air felt heavy, thick with the sound of someone unraveling. The silence became its own accomplice—watching, recording, saying nothing.

I carried the weight of two liars: my husband, who manipulated me. And my silence, which betrayed me.

The cabinet shop was supposed to be our fresh start.

Instead, it became the beginning of the end.

And before the breaking came, I looked back—toward a different woman in an unfamiliar room, a glimpse of strength I would need to remember.

❧ INTERLUDE—SHE BELONGED TO THE ROOM

My mother was never more alive to me than that night in Albany. She belonged to the room the way a flame belongs to its wick—bright, inevitable, impossible to ignore.

It was her fortieth high school reunion. I must have been nineteen or twenty—old enough to understand the weight of being seen, but still young enough to be dazzled by it. She invited me to come along—just me—and I don't remember if I asked or if she offered, but I said yes before the question even settled in the air.

We had moved to West Texas in 1969, and this must have been '76 or '77. By then, she had made this new community hers, too. That same energy she carried growing up in Albany—the girl who rode horses around the courthouse lawn and played football with the boys—she had brought with her. And expanded.

She and my father had become successful. They'd joined the local theater and poured themselves into it—set-building, lighting, costumes, all drawn from their Fandangle roots. My mother could string a lighting board or glue a headdress with the same precision she used arranging cheese straws for a dinner party. She did everything with a flourish, and everything with purpose.

At home, she entertained with the grace of a high-society matron and the warmth of a Texas belle. She could greet a table of oilmen in the same breath she welcomed a neighbor in need, and she carried both with equal poise. That dual gift—of charm and command—was what I saw sharpened to brilliance the night she walked back into Albany.

After ten years away, I saw her at the height of it. Moving through the reunion hall, she laughed in bursts that pulled people closer, slipped easily into conversations with classmates, husbands, wives. She seemed to draw light toward her, filling spaces others only passed through. I watched her move like a woman in full possession of her story—radiant, certain, alive.

And then there was me—nineteen, in my second year at Baylor, outfitted in the wardrobe only she could curate. That night I wore small-checked green wool pants with a matching turtleneck sweater, my hair cut short, sleek, and grown-up. For once, I looked exactly the way I wanted to feel: beautiful. Confident. Ready to take my stage.

And Albany gave it to me. As we walked in, people turned toward her—but when they saw me, they greeted me as if I were her reflection. For a moment, I belonged to her shine, and she to mine. I loved it. Center stage. That warm ripple of recognition. It was magic—the magic that made me think maybe I carried some of her fire in my chest.

But my stage at Baylor was different. I wasn't sitting front row in lecture halls or burning the midnight oil over textbooks. I was learning how to live fast and play hard. I loved the spotlight too much—the late-night laughter, the smoky parties, the rush of attention. While she commanded a room with grace and purpose, I chased applause without direction, mistaking recklessness for freedom.

That hunger—the need to be seen, to be chosen—would make me vulnerable. Later, when a man came along with promises of devotion and grand plans whispered like destiny, I believed him. I mistook intensity for love. I mistook charm for truth. I mistook the way he looked at me—like a prize he had won—for the way my mother looked at a room: as something she could light.

She looked powerful that night. And more than that, she felt powerful. I could sense it, even then.

Somewhere in town, in the fellowship hall of the Christian church, they held the reunion—but what I remember is the hum of voices and the way it changed when she walked in. Heads turned. Conversations paused just a beat—not because she was the most beautiful woman there, but because she was the one who made it happen.

She had been behind the scenes for weeks—making calls, sending reminders, tracking down classmates no one had heard from in decades. She wasn't flashy, but she had this spark—this easy, chatty way of pulling people in. Petite, with her cropped silver hair and that powder-blue St. John knit pantsuit, she looked striking, yes, but what made people light up was her energy. She made them feel welcome. Remembered. Seen. She walked into that room like it had been waiting for her—and it had.

The men, especially, lit up around her. She wasn't flirting. That wasn't it. It was the way she saw them. She asked questions and listened for the genuine answer, not just the polite one. She remembered people's lives—who they married, what they lost, where they served. She could talk to anyone: the mayor, the mechanic, the boy who once pushed her down on the courthouse lawn. Her voice carried across the room in that familiar, lilting way, full of story and spark.

And I—nineteen and hungry for belonging—soaked it up. Watching her was like watching the outline of a map I wasn't sure how to read yet, but knew I'd need someday.

That night, someone handed me a cup of punch spiked with something stronger. JC was there too, of course, sneaking sips from his flask, laughing in the shadows like a teenager, even though he must've been pushing seventy. In Albany, reunions were less about class years and more about orbit. If you were part of someone's memory, you showed up. Age didn't matter.

People came up to me and told me stories about my mother as a girl—pigtailed and wild, riding her horse around the courthouse lawn, chasing boys. She used to play football with the fellas from the "wrong side of the tracks." She was fast, they said, and fearless. She got in trouble for it, especially with her father. But she didn't stop.

Hearing those stories, I realized that what I had seen that night wasn't new. It was a continuation—a woman grown from a girl who had always demanded to live on her own terms.

That night, I understood something I hadn't fully seen before: she had always been herself—restless, rebellious, radiant. It wasn't motherhood. It wasn't marriage. And it wasn't grief that shaped her. It was her—always her—the way she gathered people to her like light drawn to flame. The way she made people feel known.

I stored that version of her like a keepsake. Tucked it deep in my mind, into a room colored in gold and sun and silk. A room I could walk into later, when everything turned gray.

Before the silence. Before the illness. Before the rift that took her away from me piece by piece.

That night, she was still whole. And so was I.

And for just a little while—before everything faded—she belonged to the room.

And she belonged to me.

CHAPTER 18:

THE SLOW FADE

BONES BENEATH THE PRAIRIE
Roseann Mayer

Part I

There were moments that almost felt like grace—tiny reprieves, like sunlight slipping through a cracked door. Before the fatigue. Before the silence. Before the fury. We still had those.

During those years, my parents came to Houston often for business. They stayed in the company's suite downtown, a place that smelled faintly of leather and polished mahogany, where the carpet hushed every step. Sometimes my mother would call and invite me to join them—just me, or me and the children. We'd dress for the occasion and go to high tea at The Hedges inside Neiman Marcus, where white china clinked softly and the servers addressed her as "Mrs." with reverence born of long-standing loyalty. Or we'd dine at the Petroleum Club, surrounded by oil men in dark suits and women in silk, as if the children and I belonged in that world.

She always came dressed like royalty—pearls, a perfectly pressed suit, heels that clicked like punctuation on the marble floors. She made sure the children looked the part, too: monogrammed jumpers, stiff shoes, toys piled in the suite while our own bank account scraped bottom. My daddy laughed and went along, quiet but pleased, patting their heads while my mother ordered for the table with the authority she'd carried all her life.

I played my part, smiling at the right moments, spinning stories about custom cabinetry and fine homes. All of it is true—just curated. Neat. Polished. Successful. For a few hours, I could pretend we were one of those families—whole, well-dressed, put together. I accepted their compliments, their praise, and let the illusion stand. But inside, I was unraveling. Behind the lipstick and linen, behind those downtown lunches, my world was collapsing.

Those polished moments shimmered like pearls strung across a fraying thread. Lovely, yes—but fragile. And I knew deep down they wouldn't hold.

One evening, I sat across from my mother in the suite's sitting room. The lamps cast a warm golden light, softening the hard edges of her face. She sipped her coffee, smoothed her skirt, and for a moment it felt as if the old rhythms were still there, waiting.

But then came the fatigue.

Not mine—though I had plenty of it. Hers. The kind that settled behind the eyes, hollowed the cheeks, quiet but insistent. She brushed it off: just a rash, she said, something minor the doctors were watching. But her voice betrayed her—too light, too practiced. I knew my mother. Something was deeply wrong.

When they finally ran the scans—just to be safe—it wasn't reassurance that came back. It was the word we all feared:

Breast cancer.

And all the while, the storm between them and me raged on. My father called constantly—demanding explanations. What was going on with the books? Why was he lying? Why was I letting him? I had no good answer. Only guilt. Only dread.

Five or six months later, my cousin—the oncologist—called me and my sister. His voice was calm, but the words hit like a freight train: the cancer was aggressive, a fire raging in her body. She was still in denial, clinging to hope, but we knew then—she probably didn't have long.

I drove to West Texas that afternoon. She opened the door in full makeup, a scarf tied neatly at her neck, perfume lingering in the air. She looked like a woman headed to a luncheon, not one facing surgery. She smiled as if we were still fine—still mother and daughter, not strangers made brittle by distance and years of disappointment.

I still adored her. Even after everything—even after the screaming and silence and judgments—I wanted her to be proud of me. I wanted to crawl into her lap and cry like I was ten again. But I couldn't. I had children. A business. A thousand secrets.

She asked little about the shop. Maybe she was too tired. Maybe she already knew.

That night, I sat in the kitchen alone while the house slept. The silence pressed in, and I realized: I was losing her. Not just to cancer, but to time. To all the things we never said. To everything we'd let stand between us. And I couldn't stop it.

My father never let the unraveling show. He stayed steady, insisting the treatments were promising, that she'd pull through. He had always assumed he would go first; their entire life had revolved around that belief. Their wills. Their plans. Her diagnosis fractured that story. And though he still dressed each day as if nothing had changed—suit, starched white shirt, tie fastened neatly even at the hospital—everything had. He was shattering quietly, just beneath the pressed collar.

The world looked unchanged, but nothing was.

PART II

The summer swelter that year felt heavier than usual, as if the air itself had thickened with what we weren't saying. Out in West Texas, the sun rose early and unrelenting, bleaching the sky until it was a pale, washed-out blue. Even in Houston, where the air was damp instead of dry, stepping outside was like opening the door to a steam oven.

My mother hated the heat. She always kept her home chilled, the air conditioner humming, the scent of lemon oil rising in the stillness. But even the cool air inside couldn't disguise the way summer pressed on us—slowing time, stretching every moment into something weightier.

That heaviness seeped into the hospital corridors, too. I felt it on the walk from the parking lot, hot pavement radiating through my shoes, sky bleached white above me. By the time I stepped into her room, the contrast was jarring: the sudden chill, the mechanical hum of filtered air, the sharp scent of antiseptic.

She was in bed, propped against pillows, lipstick perfect as always, as if she'd applied it for an occasion rather than a chemotherapy appointment. The scarf at her neck was cheerful, patterned in pinks and creams. She smiled like a hostess welcoming me to a luncheon instead of a woman tethered to IV lines.

But her eyes gave her away. Guarded. Calculating. As though weighing what she could say against what she couldn't forgive. We spoke in fragments—about the nurses, the flowers someone had sent, the weather. Never about the chasm between us.

Her anger still lived in the silence. Illness had claimed her strength, but not her resolve. She hadn't let go of what had happened with the business, the missing payroll, the humiliation of selling her diamond ring. To her, that betrayal was stitched onto my skin, inseparable from me.

I sat in the chair beside her bed, hands folded in my lap, posture straight—drilled into me from childhood. I prayed silently, asking God to soften her heart, to let even a sliver of grace pass between us before it was too late. But the air between us stayed cool, almost cold, despite the summer pressing at the windows.

The days blurred. I drove back and forth between Houston and West Texas, the road shimmering ahead of me, the hum of tires my only companion. I thought of the girl I had once been, the one who could crawl into her lap without hesitation, and wondered if she was gone for good.

I still loved her. I always had. But in those last months, I understood that love doesn't always melt what's hardened. Sometimes it just holds its shape—quiet, steady, present—even when it is not returned.

And so I kept showing up. Even if she never forgave me. Even if the distance stayed. Even if my place in her heart had been replaced by the ledger of our failures. I brought my prayers with me, tucked like folded letters in my pocket, believing—stubbornly—that there was still a way for God to make all things beautiful.

Even as the light dimmed around her, I kept lighting candles—small flames of faith against the dark.

Fear is what if?

Faith is even if.

And I carried that with me—steady, stubborn—into the night ahead.

And when the nights grew heaviest, I found myself reaching for other lights—earlier ones, remembered ones—that once showed me how to glow in the dark. They belonged to another time, in a babysitter's plain clapboard house on the edge of town, and to a girl who seemed lit from within, carrying a radiance I never forgot.

❧ INTERLUDE—CAROLYN, THE GIRL WHO GLOWED

Some memories stay sharp as coloring book lines—etched not just by crayon, but by awe, by longing, by the ache of who we once were in the presence of someone unforgettable. Before everything broke, there was still this: the local babysitter's house on the edge of town—crayons and Kool-Aid, and the first girl I ever idolized.

Off to Sue's house we went—Mom and a group of ladies headed to Cisco to shop for the day. The sitter's house, a white clapboard camp-style cottage, plain and practical, with what I think was just two bedrooms and one bathroom, was where all the kids gathered when mothers needed a break—sometimes just for the afternoon, sometimes overnight. But inside? It held a world of wonder.

There was a large double bed in the second bedroom where the girls took naps, the covers always pulled tight, the pillows slightly dented from the heads that had just left them. Boys got pallets—thick old quilts laid out in the living room, next to the box fan and the squeaky rocker. There was a TV in the corner, its rabbit ears wrapped in foil, but it was rarely turned on. We weren't there to watch; we were there to live, to tumble out the back screen door into a world of dirt, dandelions, and discovery.

And in the backyard—half wild, half tended—there was the 'frady hole, Texas slang for a storm cellar, tucked beneath a wooden door, its handle rusted and stiff. It terrified us all. The air that drifted up when it opened smelled like wet concrete and spiders. It was pitch dark down there, and we'd whisper ghost stories about what might live in the corners. But when a Texas storm rolled in, black and sudden, Sue would hustle us out the back door—boys, girls, all of us—to crowd into that concrete cave with our knees knocking and our hearts thudding. It was fear and safety all at once.

Sue was kind but firm. You didn't run wild. You didn't talk back. There were rules, and there were consequences—usually only a sharp word or a swat from a willow switch that hung by the back door like a warning. But it never felt cruel. It was respectful discipline laced with care, the kind that made you feel safe inside the boundaries she kept. Our parents were all for it. She was fair and fun and made a plate of fried bologna with mustard and brown sugar feel like a banquet. She'd plop pork and beans on the side, slide us a slice of white bread, pour a glass of tap water, and we were golden.

There was always a hum in that house—kids talking, crayons scraping across newsprint, the creak of the floorboards when someone ran too fast. Her little living room had no air-conditioning, just a box fan propped in a window, rattling rhythmically like a metronome while we lay belly-down on the floor coloring. Sometimes she played the record player low, sometimes she read to us in a steady, Southern cadence that made even fairy tales sound like scripture.

Our mothers gave her money for coloring books, crayons, and story records. I remember Beauty and the Beast spinning from the record player while we sat cross-legged on the floor, our crowns made of imagination, crayons in hand. We'd swap colors like trading cards and gently nudge each other for room, careful not to get in trouble for pushing or crowding.

And just when I thought the coloring books and Kool-Aid were magic enough, in walked Carolyn Jones.

She wasn't just another girl in the room; she was the girl who made the crayons seem dull and the storybooks feel suddenly too small. If the sitter's house was where imagination stretched its wings, Carolyn was the wind that made them soar.

She was two years older than me. A star. A force. The only girl I can remember fawning over. Carolyn had the lead parts in every play—school, church, Fandangle, the Nativity. She didn't just enter a room, she commanded it. Even at eight. And when we were at Sue's house, I followed her like a moon circling a planet.

She showed me how to add shadow to my coloring book pages— something I had never thought to do. And just like that, I wasn't just coloring. I was creating. Because Carolyn showed me. In that moment, something unlocked—a quiet power, a glimpse of what it meant to see the world with depth and dimension. Years later, when I picked up a pen or a brush or dared to call myself creative, I'd remember her fingers guiding mine, her voice casually teaching, as if the universe might unfold if you just learned where to press darker, and where to leave the light.

We weren't friends. I was too young. But she acknowledged me. Spoke to me. Let me orbit her world. And I loved her for it—without question or condition. She was magic, and I was her audience.

I remember how she brushed her hair—deliberate strokes with a plastic brush that made a static halo around her head. I copied everything I could without getting caught. Even her way of walking down the hallway—shoulders back, chin lifted slightly like she owned the floor— was something I tried to mimic when I thought no one was watching.

Sometimes Sue would send us out to play in the dusty backyard, a patchy stretch of Bermuda grass hemmed in by a low chicken-wire fence. Even then, Carolyn dazzled. She could hula hoop longer than anyone else, her hips swinging with natural rhythm while the rest of us giggled and dropped our hoops. She jumped rope like a champion, feet barely touching the ground, her ponytail flipping like a ribbon of light behind her.

In the late afternoon, I'd lie in bed in that back bedroom, the bodies that had just been tucked in before me warming the double bed, and gaze up at the popcorn ceiling, wondering what it would be like to be her—to glow effortlessly. To be chosen without question. To walk into a room and feel the way she made everyone else feel. As though the room had been waiting for her all along.

Carolyn was the girl who made you reach. Not just for crayons, but for courage. For confidence. In some unnamed place inside yourself, belief begins. Even at that age, I understood: some people carried the light. Others just chased it.

Years later, she got tickets to see The Beatles in Dallas. Of course, she did. She was the girl history smiled at. The kind who seemed destined for big cities and bright lights. I never knew where she went after high school, but I imagined it was someplace bold, a place with escalators and curtain calls and people who understood brilliance when they saw it.

We lost touch, as children do. Life took us in different directions— moves, marriages, names changed, memories filed away in the quiet drawer labeled "youth."

But on my sixtieth birthday, John arranged dinner at the Beehive in Albany for Carolyn and me. Carolyn walked in with her parents— two people who had once moved in the same orbit as mine, both families familiar and revered. They had seemed like oil barons to me as a child—larger than life, elegant and untouchable. I had not seen any of them for forty years. I knew Carolyn was coming, but not her parents. When I saw them, all of them, it was as if someone had reached back through time and gathered the very threads of my childhood, pulling them close enough to touch. And I cried.

No time had passed. She still had the same sparkle. That same gravity. And I? I was still her loyal admirer, basking in her brilliant light. She lit up the dining room.

We hugged like women do—shoulders in, hearts forward, eyes wet. She remembered more than I expected, and less than I had carried. But the awe within me never left. Seeing them again—her, her mother, her father—felt like someone cracked open a window to my past and let the warm breeze blow through. In that moment, I touched my childhood. I touched my parents. And everything glowed.

That dinner reminded me that even after so much wreckage—so many things lost or left behind—some parts of our story wait patiently to return. Some parts of us never stop glowing. They just need someone to walk back into the room and turn the light on again.

Some girls shine so bright you never forget where you were the first time you saw them glow.

And some lights—no matter how far away they wander—still reach us, still warm us, still whisper: You mattered. Someone saw you. Someone loved you.

That's what Carolyn gave me. Not just inspiration. Not just awe. But the memory that becomes a mirror—one that reflects the parts of ourselves we sometimes forget were ever there.

And in that mirror, for just a moment, I glowed too.

But even the brightest lights of memory can't hold back the storm when it comes. And soon, it came for us.

CHAPTER 19:

THE DEATHBED AND THE STORM

◆───◇◇◇───◆

BONES BENEATH THE PRAIRIE
Roseann Mayer

Somewhere in that painful waiting, I did something beautiful—something my sister Louise never forgave. I'd read that when death comes near, it can help to surround the person with stories—memories, love, the life they've lived. So, I asked friends and neighbors, church members, childhood classmates from Albany to send notes to my mother. Cards filled with favorite moments, the stories that made them laugh, the ones worth remembering.

And they came. Every day the mailbox filled with envelopes, each one holding a piece of her life she'd forgotten to treasure.

When she was awake, she smiled, sometimes even chuckled. When she slept, I sat beside her and read those cards aloud, planting seeds of joy in the dry soil of her last days. I believed—no, I knew—this was my way of helping her get ready. Of easing the fear. Louise didn't see it that way. She didn't want anyone to know what was happening. She stayed in denial, like Daddy. But I viewed death differently. It wasn't shameful. It was holy. A homecoming with God. I was helping pave the road.

Those cards are still with me, tucked in a small lockbox. When I miss her most, I take them out. In those pages, I can walk beside her again—through the streets of Albany, through summers and Christmases and community suppers—when she was young and full of life.

My faith had never burned brighter, but it felt like standing in a house on fire with a Bible in my hand—the flames licking around me as I clung to something eternal.

I prayed daily then—sometimes hourly. Not polite, practiced prayers, but raw ones that scraped against bone. Whispers into a steering wheel, mumbles over laundry, cries into pillows at night. I begged for time. For healing. For one more moment where she could see me and know me. Mostly, I prayed for my mother—not just for her life, but for the woman she had once been. I wasn't sure I could live without that version of her.

Back in Houston, I kept the wheels of life turning. My children were older now; our live-in helper kept things afloat while I worked and called West Texas every day. The updates were never good.

As her body failed, so did her gentleness. The fury rose inside her, bigger than ever. I didn't understand it then, but later I would learn—anger often arrives when the end does, when control slips away.

I turned to my pastor. I prayed, fasted, wrestled with Scripture. I pleaded for wisdom. I asked how to say goodbye when it might come wrapped in blame. His answer was simple: "Go anyway. Be faithful. Be brave. Let love speak louder than her pain."

We went. He and his wife drove me to West Texas, believing there might still be time for reconciliation. My ex-husband was with us but staying near the car when we went in; this was between me, my parents, and God. The road was a blur—nothing but the weight in my chest.

The cancer had ravaged her. When we walked in, Daddy and Louise were there, and Daddy's friend Jim stood quietly in a corner. Radiation and chemo had whittled her down to under eighty pounds. No hair.

No muscle. Her skin was nearly translucent, like she was halfway into the next world.

Daddy, bless him, still claimed new treatments were working. He had always expected to go first. Now he was watching his beloved wife slip away and clung to the only thing he could—hope wrapped in denial.

She stirred. Her eyes opened—not with relief, not with recognition, but with rage. They swept past my friends, who knew most of our family story except the one I'd kept hidden. My pastor, I think, suspected the truth about my marriage, though he never pressed.

The hum of the central air was the only sound in the room.

She lay propped against crisp white pillows, her frame so shrunken it seemed the bed might swallow her whole. The smell was faintly antiseptic, the way hospitals smell when the flowers have wilted and the visitors have gone.

Her eyes—sharp, unblinking—found mine.

"You embarrassed us," she said, voice thin but steady. "You put us in a situation we had never faced before. Unpaid bills—in our name. That land for the cabinet shop? He tried to swindle us out of the commission. We caught him. And you—" she paused for air, "you told us his version. You tried to make us believe it was true."

Her breath rattled, but she pressed on.

"I had to sell my diamond ring to pay the IRS. I'm done with you. You are out of my will. I will never forgive you. Leave."

The words were quiet, but they were final. A verdict.

For one dizzying second, I thought of defending him—defending myself—of telling her I had only been trying to honor my husband, to believe in my marriage. But God's voice was louder: Walk away.

Hot tears blurred my vision. My body shook so hard the pastor beside me reached out, steadying me by the arm. I turned without another word. The hum of the air followed me out.

Daddy stood frozen at the end of the bed. Louise stood smugly beside him. Jim stayed still in the corner, a silent witness. My friends caught me as I crumbled, holding me upright, helping me out the door.

In the hallway, Jim pulled me aside. "Beware," he whispered. "Your sister is no friend of yours."

It was a warning.

We stepped into the searing Texas heat. The old Chevy van was stifling, the air thick and still. We drove back to Houston in silence, the only sound the tires on the highway and the occasional muffled sniffle. I knew there would be no healing in this life from her words. But maybe—just maybe—there could be peace.

A week later, the phone rang. A hospital social worker's voice was soft, measured. "If you want any chance of reconciling, of saying good-bye, you need to come now."

I was wrecked—an emotional basket case. It was clear this couldn't be fixed, and certainly not forgiven. I packed a single bag, got in my car and drove back to West Texas, alone, arriving late but just in time to go to the hospital. It was mostly dark and quiet; her door was closed, and there was no one there. She was hooked up to every machine you can imagine, and she looked like she was disintegrating before my eyes. Tears flowed down my face as I stood in the cracked-open doorway—I didn't go in. I couldn't. She was comatose.

The next morning, the house was quiet. The scent of coffee hung in the air, and sunlight filtered gently through the curtains. My father had already left for the hospital, and the maid was moving about quietly, tidying the kitchen. I dressed slowly, heavy with sorrow, and began walking down the hallway toward the front door. Something caught my attention in the living room.

There they were.

Three tall figures sat cross-legged on the sofa, robed in white. Their stillness was unlike anything I had ever known—solemn, radiant, terrifying and tender all at once. The very air seemed to bow in their presence.

Beside me, the maid gasped. Her hand shot out, clasping mine. She was startled, trembling, but not afraid. Her Catholic faith had prepared her for this, had taught her that angels often come to usher the dying home.

We did not speak. We didn't need to. In that silence, hand in hand, we both understood.

They had come for my mother. To carry her beyond my reach, to the home she had longed for all her life.

෨

The drive to the hospital was short. I sat with her the entire day, read Scripture to her fading mind, played hymns on cassette tapes which my sister could barely tolerate—she hated all this faith stuff. I can remember her huffing out of the room when I would come in and click the music on. My dad stayed by her bedside the whole day— never left. The room was still. Her breathing was shallow. I sat again at her feet and held them. I whispered apologies. I prayed for her peace.

As the sun dipped, she slipped away. Quietly. Gracefully. God allowed me to watch her spirit slip away in peace, and I believe fully that those three white-robed angels took her home.

That night, we returned to the house. By then, word had spread— my mother was gone. Several women from her Sunday school class were already there, waiting in the living room with coffee, sweet tea, and sandwiches. It was just Daddy and me who walked through the door.

He was bent over, drained, hollowed out. I was strangely relieved. Not because I wasn't broken, but because it was done—and I knew God had walked me through it.

The living room was hushed. Conversation paused as we entered. And then—thunder cracked across the sky, lightning lit up the windows, and in perfect, eerie timing—the answering machine clicked on.

"Hi, it's a beautiful day in West Texas. This is Virginia, leave a message."

Her voice. From the grave.

We froze. And then we laughed—through the tears, the shock, the grief. It was Mom, still managing the moment.

That night, I slept deeply, with peace in my bones, as if God Himself had tucked me in.

Sunlight poured through the curtains. Coffee brewed. There was a funeral to plan—two, in fact. One in West Texas. One in Albany.

She may have left in fury, but she was sent home in glory.

In the hush that follows loss, the mind reaches not for grand gestures but for the places where love once felt simple. That night, I dreamt of light—warm, butter-yellow light—and woke with the memory of a kitchen where love wasn't something you earned. It was simply there, like air carrying the scent of bread.

In the hush that follows loss, the heart goes searching—not for answers, but for places that once felt like home. Mine carried me back to a butter-yellow kitchen where love waited at the table, steady as bread cooling on the counter.

❦ Interlude—Miss Thelma's Kitchen

Before I ever knew what love felt like, I knew Miss Thelma's kitchen in Albany.

It wasn't grand—just four walls with faded wallpaper and cabinets painted butter yellow—but to us, it might as well have been a palace. The air always smelled sweeter there. The rules felt softer. And the universe tilted ever so slightly toward joy.

There was always something baking. Always. Yeast rolls or peach cobbler, sweet potato pie with a pinch of nutmeg, or yellow cake slathered in warm chocolate frosting. The radio on the shelf hummed low—Mahalia Jackson if the timing was reverent, Conway Twitty or Patsy Cline if it was a Saturday and spirits were light. Sometimes, Miss Thelma would hum along, her voice a velvet lullaby wrapping around us like warm cotton.

A pitcher of red Kool-Aid stood sweating on the counter. Cookies cooled on wax paper—vanilla wafers, chocolate crinkles, or soft molasses buttons dusted in sugar. Four little girls circled like bees in a sugar wind—barefoot, sun-browned, wild with summer.

She drove a green 1959 Ford two-door sedan, long and smooth like a land yacht. We could hear it coming before it turned the corner—its muffler purring, its paint gleaming like it had never seen a dirt road. A tall poplar stood watch beside her garage, which was always open—like her kitchen, like her arms, like her heart. We never used the front door. We came through the garage, always knocking first. That was the rule. That's what young ladies did.

The kitchen door opened straight into her world of warmth and grace. Inside, the air wrapped around you like a handmade cotton quilt from another time—cinnamon, sugar, and something deeper, something like safety. The swamp cooler in the hallway clattered and sighed, pushing out damp air that never quite cooled the house, but somehow made it feel alive.

Bette and Sandy's bedroom was just to the left, its single window shaded against the West Texas sun. The shared bathroom was simple and spotless. But it was the kitchen that held the magic. We knew it. Miss Thelma knew it too.

She let us stir the batter, even when our hands were sticky. She let us dip spoons and lick them clean. And when the cornbread rose golden and proud, she'd break off a corner, press it into my palm, and say, "Hot bread for a hot little mess."

Her kitchen was a church to me. The linoleum cool beneath our feet, the scents rising like incense, the sunlight catching in flour dust suspended midair like tiny particles of grace. It was sacred in the way only a child can understand—where love didn't need words to be real.

Even when my mom warned us not to go over, worried we'd wear out our welcome, we found our way. I think she knew. I think she remembered what it felt like to be loved like that by someone not required to love you.

Sometimes the thing your mom tells you not to want is the very thing your soul is starving for.

Miss Thelma always dressed as if she had somewhere to be, even if she did not. She wore slacks and a blouse that were crisp. Her heavily teased hairdo never drooped. Her lipstick was red, her nails immaculate, and her earrings always matched—even if she never left the kitchen. She was elegance and order, wit and warmth, rolled into one woman who made you feel like royalty, even if you were just a girl with skinned knees and tangled hair.

Every Thursday, the Avon lady came calling. Miss Thelma would let us dig through the leftover samples—tiny lipsticks no bigger than your pinky, pastel perfume vials with delicate caps, little pots of cold cream. We'd line up in front of her hallway mirror, dabbing our wrists and lips, pretending we had secrets. Pretending we were women with plans, with church hats and high heels waiting in another room. The scent of Skin So Soft and bubblegum lip gloss still lingers in my memory like a hymn.

Miss Thelma's house wasn't just the place next door. It was where I learned that sweetness doesn't always come from sugar. It comes from being seen. From being welcomed. From being chosen by someone who didn't *have* to choose you.

Even now, when cornbread bakes in my oven or Kool-Aid chills in my fridge, I'm right back there—barefoot on cool linoleum, my smile stained red, gospel humming in the background, and my heart full of the joy that only comes when someone is truly glad to see you walk through their door.

That was love. That was Miss Thelma's kitchen.

And I've been chasing that feeling ever since.

❦

Years later, I walked back into Albany with that same longing tucked inside me—craving the steadiness Miss Thelma once gave, knowing I would need it now more than ever. Albany had always been my safe place, my compass. But this time, I carried sorrow with me, and even Albany felt different under its weight.

Chapter 20:

The Funeral and the Will

BONES BENEATH THE PRAIRIE
Roseann Mayer

We had driven straight from the West Texas service to Albany; the miles unspooling like a ribbon through parched pasture and wind-twisted mesquite. By the time we pulled into the gravel circle of Gran's driveway, the afternoon sun was low and golden, casting long shadows over the clipped hedges. The air carried a familiar heat—thick and dry, laced with sweetgrass, cedar, and the faint mineral tang of caliche dust.

Somewhere, a screen door slammed. A dog barked in the distance. For a flicker of a moment, it could have been summer vacation. I could almost hear my children's laughter from years past—the slap of bare feet on wet grass, the sprinkler hissing in its slow arc while cousins squealed and darted through the spray. Once, my daughter had pressed a dandelion into my palm and whispered, *Blow it slow so your wish comes true.*

Gran's kitchen would have been waiting then—iced tea in sweating Mason jars, cornbread cooling on the counter, her perfume lingering like an embrace. We would have gathered on the back porch to watch for the next car pulling into the drive, each arrival greeted with hugs and hollers.

But this was different. This time, the reunion was for one last good-bye. The problems in my life, the noise and hurt of recent years, seemed far away in that moment. My focus was on honoring her.

I stood in the backyard, the cicadas' song a steady chorus, the breeze nudging the pecan branches overhead. The light turned the brittle grass to molten gold. For the first time in days, there was no fire to put out—just the holy pause before goodbye.

Months earlier, we had buried my grandmother—my mother's mother—at ninety-one, beside my grandfather in the Albany cemetery. Now my mother would lie beside her. One generation slipping softly beneath the soil to join the last.

Inside, the air held memories just beneath the surface. A refrigerator hummed. A ceiling fan creaked. The house knew.

My mom had asked to be buried in Albany, next to her parents. She never said why, but I knew—her heart had never really left Shackelford County. She had lived her whole life there. The Fandangle had been hers since 1938. She danced beneath the stars, learned to fly at sixteen, rode sidesaddle, judged homecoming floats, and served on the school board with grit and heels. It was the only place she truly belonged. The only place she could rest.



We'd held the West Texas service two days earlier at First Baptist Church—grand, formal, heavy with flowers and rehearsed choir numbers. The casket was closed. Louise insisted. I had barely spoken to her since our mother's final breath. I stood tall, smiling when I had to, anchoring the family through the rituals of loss. It was how I survived.

Here in Albany, I could breathe. We greeted guests that evening at the funeral home, the low hum of conversation wrapping around me like old quilt. The next morning, we gathered at the cemetery.

Folding chairs waited under a wide awning for family, the cream-and-navy programs stacked neatly on a table.

The heat pressed close, but a soft breeze moved through the live oaks, lifting the scent of roses, peonies, and gardenias from the casket spray. People came from all over—oilmen, school board members, church friends, and a few who had driven clear across Texas. They stood shoulder to shoulder along the dry cemetery road, faces shining in the sun.

I'll Fly Away—one of her favorites—rose over the crowd. As my Baptist pastor friend spoke, his voice steady and warm, I scanned faces: an old rancher dabbing at his eyes with a handkerchief, a woman mouthing every word of the hymn, a young man in a starched white shirt and pressed jeans standing with his hat clutched to his chest.

When they lowered her casket—draped in roses and bandanas, the barbed wire catching the light—I stepped forward. My hand found the edge of the wood, just for a second. I'm here. I love you.

&

Then my cousin began an a cappella chorus of Prairie Land from the Fandangle. The sound was thin at first, trembling on the wind, then it swelled—row by row, voice by voice—until the whole prairie was singing. By the second verse, it felt as if the sky itself had joined in. A lump rose in my throat. The song was Albany's heartbeat, rising through the grass, carried in every breath of those gathered, and in that moment it was hers too. But beneath the grief, something else caught flame inside me. The words branded themselves into my chest, fierce and unrelenting, as if the land itself was calling me home. It wasn't only her anthem. It was mine—burning, waiting, unextinguished.

&

Afterward, we gathered in the basement of Main Street Baptist Church. Prime rib from the Esfandiary brothers of Beehive fame, iced tea poured into red plastic cups, a few silver serving pieces gleaming under fluorescent light. Laughter rose in pockets of conversation. I stood near the back by a display of black-and-white photos, scrapbooks, and Fandangle programs, watching her life unfold in snapshots. Opinionated. Fierce. Beloved.

It was everything she had wanted. Maybe even more.

ॐ

Albany had given me that one last gift—the song, the gathering, the laughter. But two days later, we were back in West Texas for the reading of the will. That's when the peace ended. That's when the aftershock hit.

The papers were spread across the table, crisp and final. My name was there, but next to it: removed.

She had left everything to my dad, with a handwritten codicil—outlining how she wanted personal items divided between Louise and me. It wasn't legally binding, but she had spoken to Louise privately, trusting her to carry it out.

My father said little that day, but his quiet dignity steadied the room. It could have been harsher. Instead, something softer—something like grace—touched it. Painful, yes, but not cruel. My name was missing from any future claim, but it wasn't about the things. It was about the absence.

The last line of the will simply said: She knows why.

I did. But that didn't make it hurt less.

They divided the estate, signed the papers, and adjourned. Just like that, she was gone for good. And I had to begin again.

And when grief strips everything bare, memory rises sharper. The present was too stark, so my mind reached backward—toward the places where she shimmered most vividly, where she seemed untouchable. For me, that was always the Fandangle. The stage. The dress. The way a town leaned forward when she appeared, as if she carried its history on her shoulders.

❧ INTERLUDE—THE GREEN-AND-BLACK FANDANGLE DRESS

One of the best parts of April and May had always been Fandangle rehearsals at the Prairie Theatre. My mother rode sidesaddle, of course, but that didn't require practice—just a strong back, a pretty costume, and a quiet command of the spotlight. She seemed born for it, for that moment under the lights when the audience held its breath and she held their gaze.

The rest of us, though, spent those weeks jostling for parts, waiting to see who we might get to become under those wide, dusty stars. Rehearsals meant every hallway and corner was alive—men in cowboy boots clomping across the stage, women checking scripts and adjusting hats, kids running lines half-heartedly while trying to overhear the grown-ups' banter.

One year, I had my heart set on only one part: the girl in the green-and-black-striped dress. Carolyn Jones had worn it the two years before, and to me it was the pinnacle—elegant, mysterious, perfect. That dress meant thigh-high black stockings, little black shoes with a delicate strap, and the air of someone bold enough to own the stage.

That year came and went, and they didn't choose me.

During those April and May evenings, while the adults blocked scenes, repaired sets, and readied the pageant—including that whiskey-drinking scene with the fake rattlesnake I loathed—the kids were packed off to the local babysitter I've told you about before. Carolyn would be there, full of promise and theatrical flair, a kind of small-town celebrity to me. She taught me how to say the lines, how to turn my head just so, and whispered how "very hard" the part was to get. She had the voice for it—rich, deliberate, dripping with importance. I believed her.

By the following spring, my longing had sharpened. This would be my last shot. When my mother quietly told me I'd been passed over again, it was like swallowing a stone.

Tradition meant we still went to the Icehouse for costumes. It was a green hulk of a building, sitting caddy-corner from the courthouse and just across from First Christian Church—about as close to the center of town as anything could be. To me, as a child, it seemed to tower over the square. At one end was a massive sliding door and a raised loading dock, where the breeze smelled of oil and rust and something faintly sweet from years gone by.

Inside, there were always stray parts of old sets leaning in the shadows, like ghosts from shows past—a chipped saloon sign, a painted sunset backdrop, and that ten-foot-tall rattlesnake I hated with all my heart. It was paper-mâché, but it slithered unnervingly across the stage when someone hidden behind a fake rock pulled its wire. The head would lift, the tail would rattle, and the man onstage would sing that whiskey song, "Just a little and not too much, I never drink more than just a touch!" The audience howled every time, but I sank in my seat.

By Fandangle season, the Icehouse became a backstage kingdom. Racks of costumes crowded every aisle—calico skirts, cavalry coats, beaded dresses, leather chaps. Long folding tables overflowed with hats, boots, belts, and beadwork. Women I'd known all my life worked in a steady hum of hemming, pinning, and gossiping. Their laughter seemed to rattle the rafters as much as the snake's tail.

I stood in the middle of it all, trying not to sulk. My eyes kept drifting.

And then I saw it.

The green-and-black-striped dress. Hanging just above the fitting room curtain, as if it had been set there for someone else's story.

My mother steered me back to the brown cotton dresses and moccasins—my "young Indian girl" costume for the fourth year in a row. I knew the drill: hand over my shorts and shirt, try not to wrinkle the cotton shift, step into the worn moccasins, smile politely. I disappeared behind the curtain, hot tears threatening.

Then—something shifted.

The curtain slipped open just an inch. My mother's hand appeared, holding the dress. *The* dress. She said nothing, but I saw the corners of her mouth lift. The women around her were smiling too, their sewing paused, their eyes soft.

I slipped it on. It fit as if it had been waiting for me. And I—awkward, hopeful, certain I'd been invisible—burst into tears.

It remains one of the few true surprises she ever gave me. Not a gesture wrapped in conditions, not a gift laced with a lesson. Just a yes.

A dress. A moment. A mother's quiet magic.

And I have never forgotten.

I didn't know then how rare her yeses would be, or how much I would need to remember this one in the years ahead.

✦ INTERLUDE—THE SECRETARY

If my mother could conjure miracles out of fabric and insistence, Gran left her miracle standing in oak and glass. It waited in the front room, the first thing you saw when you stepped through her door. Tall and upright, carved in oak that glowed like prairie earth after rain, the Eastlake secretary held its place with quiet authority. Its hand-blown glass reflected the sun in wavy panes where tiny bubbles floated, as though fragments of air had been trapped a century ago and now shimmered like stars each time the light passed through.

This was no ordinary piece of furniture. Gran told me it had once belonged to Berta Hart Nance, the Texas Poet Laureate whose poem "Cattle" still opens the Fort Griffin Fandangle each summer. The desk carried not only oak and joinery but also the weight of words: Nance's famous lines written in her own hand, "Other states were carved or born, Texas grew from hide and horn." Alongside it was a letter of authenticity, proof of origin, folded and kept like scripture. When Gran bought the secretary in the 1940s, she was buying more than a desk. She was buying history, lineage, and a promise that words could outlast us all.

I was in fourth grade when I first pressed my fingers to the carved edges, already a child who lived inside books, already in love with English class. Gran would stand beside me, her hand resting firm on my shoulder, and nod toward the desk. "Someday you're going to write a book there," she'd say. It wasn't a wish. It was a prophecy.

When she died in 1995, the desk came to me. I had it crated and shipped, and when I set it in my great room, it was as if a piece of her voice had arrived too. Each day I would pass it, trailing my hand along the oak, the bubbles in the glass catching the light like tiny prayers. The secretary became more than an heirloom. It was an altar.

But prophecy has its own timetable. I did not write a book there while Gran was alive. When the words finally came, years later, they did not rise from the oak surface but from other tables, other keyboards. And yet, her promise held. The desk had carried the weight of faith until I was ready to carry it myself. Like the prairie that keeps its bones hidden beneath the grasses, the secretary kept the story safe until it was time to tell.

In 2020, when we retired and moved to Mexico, I faced the hardest decision. I sold the secretary—and its story—back to my cousin in Albany. It belonged there, in the soil of its origin, in the same town where Berta Hart Nance had once bent over its oak surface, and where Gran had rooted her home. Letting it go was a closing of the circle, a return of words to the place they first belonged.

Now, when I think of it, I do not see only oak grain or cubbies or bubbles in glass. I see Gran, her hand on my shoulder, whispering to a fourth-grade girl who hadn't yet believed: "Someday, you'll write a book at that desk."

And she was right. Because what matters is not the desk itself, but the faith it carried—faith that words endure, that history breathes in objects, that stories rise from beneath the surface. The desk was oak, yes, but it was also marrow, lineage, prophecy. It was proof that even when the will stripped me bare, there were other inheritances waiting—quiet, steadfast, shining like bubbles in glass, like bones beneath the prairie.

But symbols can't cook supper or warm a bed. They cannot stop the hollow from echoing once the mourners go home. And yet, even with that promise in oak and glass, what lay ahead was not steadiness but the long unraveling of what was left.

The secretary's story closed like a circle, but my own was about to split wide open. What waited was not stability, but silence—the kind that settles after the casseroles are gone and the house itself feels stripped bare.

CHAPTER 21:

WHAT'S LEFT

❖◇❖

BONES BENEATH THE PRAIRIE
Roseann Mayer

The next day, the house in Albany was still. Not the stillness of reverence, but the kind that comes when someone has scooped out something essential. The laughter, the casseroles, the ice clinking in tea glasses—gone. What remained was a silence that pressed rather than comforted.

My mother was gone. My grandmother had died nine months earlier. The house felt stripped bare, emptied of personality. The wallpaper still held its pattern. The curtains still swayed in the breeze. But the life inside had evaporated.

Something in me shifted under the weight of her passing—not just in my family, but in the marrow of who I was.

The funeral had come and gone. The tent folded. The flowers were already bowing in the sun. Those who mattered most had been there—Bette, Sandy, my mother's bridge club friends, high school friends, neighbors from long ago. The rest—faces I barely knew or hadn't seen in decades—came out of love or respect, not just for her, but for us.

They had loved her in many forms: a woman in pearls, a fierce school-board crusader, even a reluctant churchgoer who somehow commanded every room. They carried their own memories of her, fragments of a woman I would never entirely know.

No one brought up the hospital. Or the trust. Why would they? That wasn't the time.

I sat through the service in sunglasses, genuinely mourning my mother. We had our differences, yes, but I had been crazy about her. At one time, we were close. I was proud of the life she lived. Proud of the goodbye we gave her. The flowers, the music—it was exactly as she would have wanted, and for those few hours I could rest inside that truth.

Daddy collapsed inward after the burial. People whispered, laid hands on his arm, spoke in that polished cadence reserved for widowers and deacons. But I saw it—he was bracing. She had left him everything. And for me, nothing.

&◆

But that wasn't the whole of it. Because before Albany, before the burial, there had been the will. The truth had already been written down, stamped, and read aloud in a West Texas room where my name disappeared from the page.

Back in West Texas a few days earlier, I stood in the hallway near the dining room as the lawyers explained. Everything was in the generation-skipping trust. The one exception: she had removed me. The house, the accounts, the land—all locked in instruments that no longer bore my name.

My father sat still, nodding. I nodded too. Reflex.

My sister stood by the fireplace like a sentry, arms folded, eyes fixed on some point beyond me. She hadn't looked me in the eye since the night Mother died.

That same night, after the house quieted, and the children slept in borrowed beds, I sat in my father's house—where my mother had thrived, where I had just been disowned—and I had to ask him the very questions he had been asking me before she passed. About the money. The unpaid taxes. The accounts my mother had uncovered. The accusations—whispers of hidden income, IRS letters, phone calls that arrived before her death.

My ex told me it was spiritual warfare. That the devil was using my parents to divide us. That God was on our side.

I sat there hollowed out, unraveling, wondering if I had always known. Maybe I had. Maybe part of me had carried the truth like a splinter under the skin—ignored until it festered.

Grief makes everything slippery—memory, truth, even anger. I didn't cry that night. Not for her. Not yet.

Instead, I watched the door click shut behind the last mourner and moved through the house like a ghost. I tucked the children in. I turned off the lights. I stared at the grandfather clock—a Herschede, grand and gorgeous, with chimes that had marked births and deaths—still ticking, steady, as if nothing had changed.

At the sink, I reached for a bone-china mug covered in hand-painted birds. Hers. I turned it slowly in my hand. I had forgotten it until then—but in my grip, she returned in a way no photograph could. It was the mug she always filled with Sanka, heating it in the microwave, sipping slowly at the kitchen table, flipping through *Southern Living* or peeling oranges for the grandkids.

It still smelled faintly of stale coffee and cinnamon.

I didn't drink from it. I just set it gently in the dish rack, like something sacred, as if honoring both her absence and her presence at once.

&❧

And then it was Albany again. After the burial. After the will. After the truth had begun to crack me open.

I climbed into the guest bed in my grandmother's house. Silk shantung, heavy drapes. A Pack 'n Play by the bed. My ex-husband—still legally my husband—lay on the far side, pretending to sleep.

My father hadn't wanted him there. Neither did I.

But he was.

His cologne clung to the linens. His voice echoed in the silence. The man I once defended was now a question mark in the dark.

I thought about our wedding. About scripture quoted over bounced checks. About the tears he cried into my lap, spinning repentance into performance. What a masterpiece of manipulation he had woven—not just a con, but a gospel of deception, preached in sermons and sealed with tears.

I remembered the fortress I built around my marriage, brick by brick, made of hope and holy excuses. That's the thing about living with a malignant narcissist: you doubt him first, and yourself next.

That night, something cracked open. Not like a wound. Like a beginning.

I didn't know it yet, but I was already bleeding toward something new. The veil of deception was lifting. My instincts sharpened; truth gleamed like flint in dust. I had inherited my mother's fire—even if she tried to extinguish it in her last days. And with it came the courage to face what had always been in front of me.

In that bed, in that house that once held me, I finally let go of needing it.

Chapter 22:

A Crack in the Dam

◆◇◆

BONES BENEATH THE PRAIRIE
Roseann Mayer

Not sweet ones. Grackles—shrill, relentless, bickering outside the bedroom window like old women in curlers gossiping before breakfast. They were so loud it was absurd, their chatter ricocheting through the quiet of the house. For a second, I almost smiled. Almost.

Their cries cut through the hush, a jarring reminder that life, ridiculous and unrelenting, hadn't paused for grief.

Late June light slipped through the blinds in thin, uneven bands. The ceiling fan above me turned slowly, stirring air that had long since gone stale. I lay there in Gran's front bedroom, staring up, my throat dry, my eyes heavy but not from sleep. I'd made it through the graveside service without falling apart—just a few quiet tears that slipped free before I could stop them. Not enough for anyone to notice. Not enough to undo me.

᠊᠊᠊ 🙬 ᠊᠊᠊

My children—thirteen, twelve, and seven—had stood apart from me that day, each lost in their own orbit. I'd let them be. No shushing, no telling them where to stand or how to look. This was their first close loss, and it was monumental. Not a distant relative. Not a pet. This was their Gran—my mother—who had wrapped her whole life around them, doting, delighting, drawing them into her world with every ounce of her being. She spoiled them without apology, reveled in their love, built entire seasons and years around their presence.

She had plans for them. College trips in the spring. Christmas-time ski retreats. Summers at the lake. Big weddings—she already knew where the reception flowers would come from. Trips to New York for theater and tea at the Plaza. She carried those futures in her pocket like promises she couldn't wait to deliver.

And just like that—she was gone.

The memory of her burial pressed itself forward as I lay in that bed. The roses on her casket had swayed in the warm West Texas wind, their scent thick in the air, mingling with the faint tang of dust. I had kept my gaze fixed on them because looking at the dark hollow in the ground felt unbearable. I was just forty—too young to be motherless— and I knew, standing there, that I couldn't fix this for my children. Their world had cracked wide open. So had mine.

❦

Back in Gran's house that morning, the grackles outside would not stop. Their voices sawed at the edges of my resolve until something in me gave way.

I slipped from the bed without waking my kids, padded barefoot down the hallway, the boards creaking under my weight. The familiar scent of furniture polish and last night's cornbread still clung to the air. I shut myself in the back bathroom and pressed my hands to the sink.

The tears didn't roar. They crept. Slow, steady. Salt on my lips. Damp at my collar. My arms locked against the porcelain as though they were holding up the entire house.

Then came the scent—roses. Sweet and heavy, as if someone had just walked in carrying a fresh bouquet. It knocked the air from my chest. I was back at the graveside in an instant—sun burning my shoulders, the white tent fluttering in the breeze, the preacher's words slipping away into the wind.

&⁂

In the mirror, I barely recognized the woman looking back. Holloweyed. Wild-haired. Skin dull and slack. She looked like someone who'd been living in the backseat of a car. And in a way, she had.

For years, I'd sat in the backseat of my own life, letting other people drive. I handed over the wheel to men, to fear, to duty—and called it faith. I stayed when I should have run, played roles written for me by others: dutiful daughter, submissive wife, repentant sinner. All the while, my voice grew smaller, my light dimmer, my edges worn smooth.

The first crack came then, not loud, not dramatic. Just the quiet breaking of something that had strained too long.

I pressed a cool washcloth to my face, breathing in the damp cotton and the ghost of perfume I knew wasn't really there. Outside, the grackles shrieked and cackled as if mocking me—or cheering me on. I couldn't tell which.

I stayed in that bathroom a long time, studying my reflection, realizing how many years I'd spent managing everyone else's emotions, editing myself for comfort, staying small for peace. Grief wasn't just for the dead. It was for the pieces of yourself you'd buried to survive.

&⁂

When I finally stepped back into the hallway, I heard my father's voice, low and tired, speaking to Aunt Evelyn in the kitchen. The scent of coffee drifted toward me, warm and familiar, but I didn't go in. Not yet.

Instead, I curled up on the far end of Gran's floral couch in the living room, pulling the old Afghan over my knees. The couch springs creaked beneath me, the same sound they'd made when I was a child and the world felt unshakable. I stared out the window at a street that looked unchanged—lawnmowers buzzing, a dog barking, someone hammering wood down the block.

But inside me, something had shifted.

I wasn't whole. Not even close. But the story I'd been telling myself about love, about loyalty, about who I was and what I deserved—it was losing its grip.

The birds outside kept squawking.

And I kept breathing.

And the dam kept breaking.

Somewhere deep in the bones of Gran's house, the walls seemed to hold me steady—just as they had when I was a girl and the world beyond the porch felt too big.

The bones of Gran's house held me steady, but they also carried me backward. To the girl who once pressed her face to the window, half afraid, half enchanted, by the shadows beyond the cedar hedge.

❧ Interlude—The Corner Post Lamp

There was a time, back in the late 1950s in the earliest dark of December, when magic lived just past the cedar hedge.

My grandmother's house sat a half-acre back from the highway, nestled in a hush of gravel and limestone and the soft flicker of gaslight. The cedar bushes out front grew wild and low, their limbs tangled and secretive, forming a wall that made the house feel hidden from the world. As a child, I was terrified of those bushes—convinced there were snakes in their shadows, or monsters with green eyes crouched low, waiting. But just beyond that hedge, the world would shift. The gravel crunched differently. The atmosphere shifted. The magic began.

Where the circular drive met the straight one, there stood a white wooden post crowned by a gas torchiere—its flame dancing inside glass like a captured spirit. A white slat fence traced the curve of the driveway, and in the center, a limestone path led to Gran's deep-green front door. Everything matched: the carpet, the drapes, even her clothing sometimes. Green was her signature—muted but strong, like her. That door was at the heart of it all.

But in December, it wasn't the door that drew the crowds.

It was the carolers.

Not real ones. Mannequins.

Gran, a widow with grit and gumption, owned a children's dress shop beside the First National Bank downtown. Every year, she brought armfuls of mannequins home, both child-sized and adult. She'd dress them in their 1800s finery: velvet coats, bonnets, lace gloves, wool scarves, wired into place. She'd wire tiny songbooks into their hands—careful that the children's pages were lower, just so—and set them in a crescent beside the gaslight. Like a choir caught mid-verse, mid-snowfall, mid-century.

My dad and uncle helped her with the construction. My mother, my sister, and I helped dress them, pinning hems and straightening hats, like it was opening night. And it was. She rigged up a stage light—really just a workshop bulb and a dangerous tangle of extension cords—that cast an eerie, theatrical glow from below. Then she built a waterproof wooden box to house the record player and a guitar amp, placed behind the figures and hidden in the dark. Every night from six to ten, old carols would pour from that box—the scratchy kind, voices like ghosts or angels from another century. *God Rest Ye Merry, Gentlemen; Lo, How a Rose E'er Blooming; Bring a Torch, Jeannette, Isabella.*

And when the record ran out, she'd bundle up and go outside to flip it herself. Sometimes she changed records two or three times a night, always slipping into the shadows behind the mannequins as if the magic should remain unbroken.

It became a destination. This was the fifties and sixties, when evening drives to look at Christmas lights were a cherished tradition. Cars lined up along the road, headlights dimmed, toddler's faces pressed to the windows in wonder. I remember hearing their squeals through the thick glass of Gran's picture window—muffled laughter, tiny hands clapping, the thrill of believing the mannequins might really sing.

Inside, we'd sit with the lights off, our noses nearly touching the cold glass, watching like it was Broadway. Gran called it "our show." And it was. She'd serve sugar cookies shaped like reindeer and candy canes, and spin stories of her own childhood—of blizzards and horses and tinsel made from lead, of Christmases lit by oil lamps and warmed by wood stoves. She made it sound like the 1900s were a fairy tale she had survived. And maybe she had.

There were years we helped. Years we missed. But the carolers came back, year after year, through snow flurries and windstorms, through grief and change and ordinary Decembers. Until the year they didn't. Until she couldn't. But by then, it had already etched itself in us like scripture.

Sometimes now, when the world feels dark or unkind, I remember that flicker of light behind the hedge—the mannequins standing still and proud beneath the gas torchiere, the hush of wheels on gravel, the record warbling as Gran changed it with mittened hands. I remember the way our breath fogged the window and the way wonder swelled in my chest like song.

We weren't watching mannequins. We were watching hope, dressed up in velvet and pinned in place by a woman who refused to let the darkness have the last word.

It wasn't just a porch light.

It was the corner post. The lamp lit the way for all of us.

CHAPTER 23:

THE LIST

BONES BENEATH THE PRAIRIE
Roseann Mayer

By the time I made it to the kitchen the next morning, Louise had already arrived with her brood; the house had stirred. Sunlight pressed against the windows in narrow gold stripes, warming the yellow linoleum floor. Daddy sat at the breakfast table, a half-eaten piece of toast on his plate, the paper folded beside him. He held his coffee mug with both hands, as if it might anchor him.

He didn't look up when I came in—just gave a soft grunt, the kind that meant: I see you, but let's not make a thing of it.

The smell of toast lingered in the air, but the toaster was already cold. A plate of scrambled eggs sat untouched on the counter with a note in my sister's slanted handwriting: Feed the kids. I went to check on the cows.

Everyone had somewhere to be but me.

I poured a cup of coffee, careful not to spill. The kitchen hadn't changed since childhood—the same copper-bottomed pots hanging over the stove, the same fridge held shut with masking tape at the corner where the seal had gone. Even the potholder drawer, still jammed too tight, squeaked the way it always had.

I sat down across from Daddy. He finally glanced up, just once, then pushed a yellow legal pad across the table toward me.

"Your mother had a list. Things she wanted taken care of. Before she ... you know."

I stared down at it. Her handwriting was unmistakable—strong, elegant, always in black ink. She wrote as she spoke: with certainty and no room for confusion. Each line was a command, not a suggestion.

There were funeral details, of course. Names to call. Hymns to use. A note that simply read: *No lilies. Roses if possible.* She had even written her own obituary draft, with edits in the margins. Her voice leapt from the page as if she were still in the room, telling me what to do and how to do it.

But halfway down the page was something unexpected.

I read aloud: "Rose bushes, trim before spring."

Daddy didn't smile, but the corners of his mouth twitched. Something in his tired, glassy eyes flickered with warmth.

His voice trembled. "She was still thinking about the house, even when she knew she wouldn't see another season."

I ran my finger along the ink. She'd listed them all: *trim the rose bushes. Take winter clothes to the church closet. Refill bird feeder.* Tucked between medical instructions and burial requests were breadcrumbs of the life she'd lived—and the life she hoped we'd keep.

The page blurred as my eyes welled. I blinked them back.

"She wanted us to be okay."

Daddy nodded slowly. "She didn't know how to show it some-times. But she did. In her way."

He reached for his coffee again, staring into the steam like he might find her there. I looked back down at the list.

There was a section labeled *For the Girls.* My breath caught.

Under my name, she had written: *The silver brush set. The quilt is from Mom. The gold locket.*

I bit the inside of my cheek. I remembered the brush set on her dresser. I used to sneak it as a girl and pretend I was a queen, brushing out my curls in the mirror when no one was looking.

Under Louise's name, she had listed: *Blue Wedgwood plate. Grandmother's teacup. Pearl brooch.*

No explanation. No sentiment. Just a quiet record of meaning.

I don't know how long we sat there—the list between us; the coffee cooling. Outside, a tractor rumbled in the distance. The screen door creaked open and shut as the kids wandered in for juice and cartoons.

Daddy folded the paper in thirds and slid it into his pocket after reading it aloud. I knew even then it would always remain unfinished.

Later, I pulled on boots and went out to the garden. The sun was already climbing, the air warming quickly. I found her unruly shrub roses by the back fence, exactly as I remembered—overgrown, wild, defiant, just like she had been. The pruning shears were still in the utility drawer where she'd kept them. I slipped on gloves and got to work.

Each cut felt like a prayer. Not for answers, but for strength.

We didn't get everything right, she and I. But this—this I could do.

Grief doesn't come with instructions.

But sometimes, if you're lucky, it comes with a list.

By the time I set the shears down, the sun was dipping low, and the air smelled of cut branches and dust. Her list was finished, but it didn't end anything—it only marked the place where I had to step forward without her. The roses stood behind me, trimmed but still wild, a kind of stubborn testimony that life would keep growing whether I was ready or not. A few days later, it was time to leave Albany again, the house quieter than ever. I carried her handwriting with me, folded and worn, as we turned back toward Houston.

CHAPTER 24:

A HOUSE WITH SHUTTERS

◆–◇–◆

BONES BENEATH THE PRAIRIE
ROSEANN MAYER

We drove back to Houston in silence, slipping into a version of life that wore the mask of healing. It was an exhausting performance, keeping up the illusion of normalcy, of progress—each smile, each chore completed, a stitch in the fabric of a life that no longer fit. Each day chipped away at something vital in me, leaving a dull ache behind my eyes and a quiet trembling in my bones. Pretending took energy I no longer had, and the cost of that deception was mounting in ways I couldn't yet name. On the surface, everything looked like it should: the steady hum of routine, the soft shuffle of backpacks and lunchboxes, the occasional laugh in the hallway. It almost worked. We were building something again—a life, a house, a business. But beneath the surface, a quiet dread pressed against the windows like a wind I couldn't block out.

The kids were half-asleep in the back seat, their heads bobbing gently with every dip in the highway. My husband's hand drummed on the wheel as he hummed along to the radio, like we were just a regular family headed home from a long weekend. I held the silence like a thin thread between my fingers; afraid it might snap. Outside, pump jacks nodded in dusty fields, and the scent of oil mingled with fast-food wrappers on the floorboards. Inside the car, the air was thick with unspoken things.

Back home, we moved through our days like clockwork. I unpacked boxes, folded laundry still smelling of storage, and simmered pots of chili. "Creative Cabinets" picked up momentum. He printed business cards with embossed logos and charmed clients as they ran their hands over smooth wood grain. In the shop, sawdust danced in shafts of sunlight. He looked the part—clean-cut, sleeves rolled, a pencil tucked behind his ear. And I stood beside him—smiling, nodding, pouring coffee, closing deals—as if nothing rotted beneath the veneer.

We even began constructing a home. A Southern Living Custom Home pulled straight from a magazine—Chicago brick, emerald green shutters, crisp white clapboard, and a generous wraparound porch made for iced tea and Sunday stories. It looked like the promise of peace, a picture-perfect symbol of everything we said we were rebuilding. But the more I stared at it, the more desperate I became for it to be real—how badly I needed something solid to point to and say, "See? We made it." The contrast between that carefully curated dream and the quiet rot beneath the surface grew harder to ignore. The place you imagine raising children, carving pumpkins, hanging stockings. A breakfast nook. A bay window where I pictured the Christmas tree would go. It looked like redemption. It wasn't.

But day by day, underneath the fresh paint and siding, I could feel the corrosion returning. I told myself it was just fatigue. That maybe all marriages had shadows. But late at night, when the children were asleep and the shop lights were off, I could feel the lies pacing. The signs crept in like mildew.

One evening, while sorting laundry, a crumpled hotel receipt slid from his pocket—rooms charged late into the night. It felt like mildew finding its way behind the drywall: slow, sour, undermining everything.

From the first night of our marriage, when he took me to a strip club on our honeymoon and called it foreplay, I had known his desires reached places I could not follow. He spoke often about the kind of sex he wanted, and as a young Christian wife I tried to believe the marriage bed was sacred, that if I yielded enough, it might be enough. I wasn't naïve; I understood more than I wished I did. But I also knew what I could never allow in my home. That tension became my cage—because rejecting what I knew was wrong meant risking his anger, and he always had the upper hand.

So when that receipt slipped into my palm, it wasn't simply evidence of betrayal; it was confirmation of a battle I had been fighting in silence for years.

There were other signs too: absences explained away as errands, whispered phone calls from the garage that cut off when I drew near, an unfamiliar scent on a jacket left where it shouldn't be. The boxes in the back room wore neat labels—"Cabinet Specs," "Design Drafts"—but the names were a veil.

One afternoon, looking for a hammer, I pried open a box tucked behind an old table saw. The tape resisted, then tore with a rip that echoed in the empty shop. The stench hit me like a slap: mildew, grease, and something worse. Inside were things that did not belong to the life I thought we were living—clothing, papers, images in a woman's hand that wasn't mine. I froze, one hand braced on the cardboard as if it could steady me. My stomach turned. My ears rang. The contents weren't just filthy; they were a dare.

It stopped being only betrayal. It became erosion—the slow wearing away of trust until the ground beneath me gave way. I snapped the box shut with shaking hands and walked back through the house as if nothing had shifted. But everything had.

He began hiding things in other places, too. One Saturday, rummaging through the glove box for insurance papers, my fingers brushed silk and glass—an expensive bottle of perfume tucked beneath registration slips, a tube of lipstick in a shade I'd never worn. Later, behind boxes filled with VHS tapes of the kids, I found a shoebox with photos that made me want to rip out my own eyes. A program from Les Misérables—a show he claimed to hate—was wedged between tax forms. I began checking everything. And with each discovery, something in me hollowed out.

I said nothing. I had known from the beginning. From our first encounter. From the way he moved through life with a slippery charm that never quite held. I had known, and I had chosen not to know. There's a difference. Knowing is one thing. Admitting is another.

A man who preached with one hand and degraded with the other. Who smiled for Christmas photos, then disappeared for hours. Who could hold my daughter on his knee while secrets stained his pockets? And me? I kept the calendar, my checkbook, the lie.

I stopped believing in the version of him I had married. And worse, I stopped believing in myself. I had built my life around something vile. And I had painted it pretty—layer by layer, with birthday candles and PTA meetings, with monogrammed towels and family photo shoots—until even I forgot what was underneath. The emotional toll was relentless, like carrying a tray of glass in a windstorm, always pretending not to flinch. I smiled so hard my face ached. I acted so well I forgot it was an act. But deep down, I knew—if I stopped pretending, the whole thing might come crashing down around us. Rocking chairs on a porch I hoped would last. A foundation built on silence and sinking sand will always crack.

At night, I would lie awake and imagine retirement with him. All I could think was how horrible that would be, and how I couldn't possibly last that long. The con he was running—on me, on the people I cared about—was destroying me. I held the truth in my gut and hated his lies, but there was no confronting him; every time I tried, he turned his back on me.

I wanted to believe the counseling sessions, the books we devoured, the date nights carved out like vows meant we were building something good from what we had broken. There were happy moments—laughter over pancakes, the kids' hands in mine, the small triumph of a sale closed—that flickered like hope. My children and the work I loved were the delight of my heart. Those bright spots were real. But they couldn't erase the dread that still throbbed beneath. I begged God for help.

I kept the motions—homework, soccer, lunchbox notes, prayers whispered over their beds, hot cocoa on the stove, curtains hemmed by hand, birthday parties with buntings and balloons. I smiled at church. I played the role. But inside, the truth was unraveling.

This is my side of the story. Whether I recall every detail with perfect clarity is something even I've questioned. But it is the lived truth as I remember it. Names and places have been changed in parts to protect the innocent and those who would rather forget. My children lived it too, and they carry scars I may never fully see. And him? He'd tell it another way. He'd say I was wrong. That I was dramatic, forgetful, unstable. Maybe I was. But this much is true: I wanted so badly for the illusion to be real that I stood in the fog and called it sunlight. I clung to the outline of a life I prayed would come into focus, even as it vanished around me.

Looking back now, I see the veil I wrapped around myself wasn't only denial—it was survival. I had learned that veiling from the women before me—my mother most of all—who bore pain with polish and silence. But even behind the curtain, the air grew heavy. The mask cracked. And slowly, like my mother before me, I saw things as they were, not as I wished them to be. Fire and clarity—her inheritance in me—burned through the mist. I had inherited her will, her discernment, her backbone wrapped in grace. Not all at once. But enough to know the dam was breaking, and that I would not rebuild it this time.

I lived in that house with shutters—every one of them closed.

And yet memory slipped through, even when the shutters stayed shut. Grief has a way of finding the cracks—seeping in through small, ordinary things, catching you off guard. That's how she came back to me, not in grand gestures, but in glimpses. One of those glimpses was a stage, a tutu, and a moment I had spent years trying to forget.

❧ INTERLUDE—THE BALLET RECITAL

After my mother died, memories of her came in waves—some sharp, some sweet, some sneaking up in the middle of a grocery aisle. Once, I caught sight of a pink can of salmon—the kind she used for croquettes—and tears spilled before I knew what had happened. Grief is like that. It doesn't follow rules. It rises from the steam of a kettle, the smell of floor wax in an old church hallway, or the first notes of a song you don't know the name of but feel in your bones.

One memory that returned, brighter than expected, was the ballet recital.

Every Southern girl took tap, ballet, or piano. These weren't just lessons; they were badges of belonging. Proof that you were being raised "right"—with thank-you notes, Sunday dresses, and monogrammed towels. For me, that meant climbing the groaning stairs above Green's Grocery, where Miss Betty Ann reigned in lipstick and pearls, teaching generations of Albany girls how to point their toes and keep their heads high.

The studio smelled of dust and lacquered hair, a haze that followed us up the creaking stairs. The floors held the echoes of a thousand pirouettes. I was never the graceful one—long-limbed, awkward, with a smile that gave away my nerves. Truth is, I loved the costumes more than the discipline. The satin slippers, the pale pink tights, the layers of tulle that floated like spun sugar—I wanted to wear them every day. The sparkle of sequins, the hush before the music, the way lights transformed us into something more than little girls—that's what I loved. The dance steps? That was the price of admission. What I really wanted was the stage, with all its promise of transformation. I thought the stage would be magnificent—and it was, even when I failed on it.

That night, it was my turn. Albany High's auditorium was packed—neighbors, cousins, church ladies in their Sunday dresses, the whole town, it seemed. The curtain rose. I stepped out in my tutu, sequins glinting, cheeks rouged, heart pounding. For a moment, the light was everything I'd hoped for: warm, dazzling, magnificent.

Then the music began.

And my mind went blank.

Every practiced move scattered like a flock of birds startled into the sky. I couldn't remember a single step. I knew I couldn't just stand there. I knew I couldn't walk off. So I did the only thing I could think of: I turned.

Across the stage I whirled, a small figure caught in motion under too-hot lights, sequins flaring like sparks. It wasn't choreography. It wasn't art. It was survival. My body was moving because stillness felt unbearable. Three long minutes of improvisation—circling, wavering, trying to keep pace with music my mind had lost.

When it was over, the applause was polite but thin, the kind that comes more from pity than delight. I felt it in my skin—the difference between clapping for a triumph and clapping because the child hadn't fled the stage in tears. Small towns remember things like that. They don't speak of them, but they tuck them away, and you feel it the next time you walk into the Piggly Wiggly or down the church aisle.

Later, my mother's face told me I'd embarrassed her. But what imprinted most wasn't the sharpness of her words—it was the silence that followed. The heavy quiet in the car, the way she wouldn't meet my eyes. I carried that silence like a bruise into other rooms of my life, always aware of how quickly love could turn to judgment, how easily belonging could be withdrawn.

Still, when I return to that night now, I don't remember only the shame. I remember the costume, the heat of the lights, the blur of sequins against velvet curtains. I remember how much I loved the stage, even when the stage betrayed me—or maybe when my mind did. That was the first time my brain failed me, and I felt the terror of being seen with nothing to give.

I never danced another solo. I slipped into the ensemble, safer in the shadows, where no one expected me to carry the music alone. But I never lost the craving for the moment before the curtain rises—the hush, the breathless possibility, the sense that transformation might happen if only you're brave enough to step forward.

Years later, I felt the same sensation in another kind of spotlight— the stage of my marriage. I wanted the costume, the part, the glow of belonging. I wanted to play my role well enough that no one would see the panic underneath. And when memory failed—when love soured, when cruelty replaced tenderness—I did the same thing I'd done as a girl. I improvised. I kept moving so no one would know I'd forgotten the steps.

Looking back, that recital was more than a child's embarrassment. It was a rehearsal of what was coming. The pressure of performance. The weight of an audience's eyes. The desperate turning when your mind goes blank and you can't find the choreography.

And yet, there is tenderness in the picture too. A girl in pink satin shoes, dizzy but unwilling to stop, sequins flashing like stars. She deserved applause—not for perfection, but for staying on the stage.

Even now, when I catch the scent of hairspray or hear the swell of an orchestra tuning, I return to her. Not with shame, but with reverence. She was awkward, afraid, improvising.

But she was also luminous.

She stepped into the light.

And for one magnificent moment, she danced.

Years later, I would watch my father's new wife step into her own role—graceful where my mother had been unruly, polished where I had once spun in panic. She wore the part with ease, as if she had been preparing for it all her life. And once again, I felt the weight of an audience's gaze, measuring who belonged and who did not.

CHAPTER 25:

THE SECOND WIFE

BONES BENEATH THE PRAIRIE
Roseann Mayer

Daddy's wedding came quickly.

I suppose it always does when you're sixty-eight and a recent widower. You don't stand around parsing grief—you find the woman who knows how to refill your glass, mend your socks, and keep the house smelling of lavender sachets and lemon Pledge. A woman whose refrigerator holds Blue Bell in a plastic tub and ham salad marked with masking tape, the date written in tidy block letters.

Her name was Jane. Kindness and goodness defined her. Jane showed poise and warmth and always knew just what to say. She brought over casseroles without asking and remembered birthdays without reminders. She made my daddy smile again. Laugh again.

They had known each other for years—family friends, the couple you vacationed with when you still had children at home. Her first husband, Dan, divorced her after forty-five years of marriage for a younger woman, and in that rupture, she learned the quiet ache of abandonment—something my father understood all too well after my mother's long illness and death. Jane was no stranger to grief. My father needed someone who could step in with little instruction. Someone who already knew which drawer held the kitchen scissors and which neighbor to call when the dogs got loose.

They held the wedding in the church parlor at First Baptist in West Texas, a town where I now felt like a guest. It was small, quiet, tasteful. Daddy wore a pale blue tie and looked tired but polished. My children sat beside me, fidgeting, confused. I kept folding and unfolding the program in my lap, as if it held answers I was missing. The flowers were modest. No peonies, no bandanas, no barbed wire—just lilies, Gran, and the faint scent of a new chapter I wasn't ready for.

Afterward, we gathered at the country club—hers and ours—for a grand luncheon with champagne and caviar. The silver gleamed. White-jacketed servers moved effortlessly among us with trays of crab-stuffed mushrooms and cheese straws. Someone played an old Sinatra song on the piano—the very one my mother used to hum while rinsing dishes at the sink.

It almost undid me. I pressed my napkin into my lap, willing myself not to cry in front of a roomful of polished strangers. The surrounding laughter grew louder, but I felt a thin veil drop, as if I had slipped into another world where my mother was already fading, and Jane's smile filled the space she had left.

Jane greeted everyone with her gracious drawl and perfect posture. She looked beautiful in pale lavender, with a smile on her face that said she believed in happy endings. And perhaps it was that very grace—so easy, so seamless—that felt foreign to me. Her ability to move forward without hesitation, to beam with such serene certainty, made me feel like an outsider in a story I hadn't finished grieving.

It wasn't her fault. She knew I wasn't ready, and she never pushed. She met me with patience, never hurrying my steps, never shaming me for the way I lingered in closets and drawers, touching the clothes and shoes my mother had left behind. She understood that the scent of Tea

Rose on a dresser could be an anchor, that a bathrobe hanging from the back of a door might feel like a lifeline. She let me grieve at my own pace.

Despite that, the shift was undeniable. One by one, the pieces of furniture disappeared—tables, chairs, lamps—each carrying more than wood and fabric. They held her charisma, her charm, the memory of rooms made brighter by her laughter, and her uncanny ability to make anyone feel welcome. Their absence left me unmoored, as if the air itself had changed.

Jane never erased my mother. She couldn't. What she did was bring light where shadows had settled. She knew how to ease my father's loneliness, how to fill the silence with warmth rather than demand. She made him smile again, laugh again. She gave him something to live for when grief might have otherwise swallowed him whole.

And I loved her for that. Even when it hurt. Even when my heart wasn't ready.

We knew Daddy would close up the family home and move into Jane's house. That meant dividing up my mother's things, and yes, there was a list for that too. My name was still on it—maybe she'd forgotten to take it off. Still, walking through the rooms of my childhood, watching pieces of her life—our life—boxed and labeled felt like a slow dismantling of everything sacred. I didn't cry. I didn't rage. I just went numb.

Still, she made him happy. That was undeniable.

They moved into her townhouse, carefully decorated with pale florals and polished brass. When we visited, everything was just so—casseroles warming in the oven, birthday cards already stamped, everyone's favorite dessert waiting on the counter.

I wanted to let her in. I tried.

But there was something about watching my father fall in love again—after all we'd been through, after all my mother had endured—that made me feel like a stranger in my family.

Not because Jane did anything wrong.

She did everything right.

She dropped off pies she had baked from scratch with no fanfare. She always sent handwritten thank-you notes, and she knew how to fold hospital corners on a bed. She seemed to float through grief with grace, her every gesture a quiet promise that life could be lovely again. And somehow, in doing all of that with such serene precision, she revealed how much of my mother's charisma and presence had been singular, irreplaceable. Jane didn't dim it—she illuminated the absence.

It was the evening after the wedding and luncheon when I went to their new home for the first time. Jane greeted me in the doorway with her usual smile. The air inside smelled of lavender sachets, cinnamon, and my dad's pile of newspapers in the corner. On the entry table sat a framed photo from their wedding—Daddy beaming, Jane holding a small bouquet.

There was nothing of my mother in sight. No carved walnut frame, no familiar image watching from its place by the door.

I stood there longer than I should have. Just long enough for the smile on Jane's face to falter.

"Come in, sweetheart; your dad is in the den."

I stepped over the threshold, but something stayed behind—some part of me loyal to her memory, to the version of home that smelled like lasagna and Tea Rose perfume, that whispered soap opera storylines and theater organ anthems, that still waited for someone to notice me. Some part of me, still curled up on the green couch at our old house, watching *As the World Turns* with my mother, hoping she'd glance over and notice how pretty I looked that day. Hoping she'd say it out loud.

She never did.

And neither did he.

But he smiled a little more with Jane. He laughed again. He walked straighter.

He lived.

And I suppose that's what a second wife is for.

Still, there were places in his life that no one else could touch—territory that belonged to the years before, to the version of him who was just my daddy. One of those places was the oil patch.

❧ INTERLUDE—THE OIL PATCH RIDE

We weren't allowed to go to Daddy's rig sites often, but when we did, it felt like being smuggled onto a movie set—one with its own script, cast, and spotlight. The moment he lifted me into his huge Lincoln—the one with the blue leather seats warm from the sun—I felt chosen. That car gleamed like a ship under the Texas sky, chrome edges flashing as if the horizon itself were sending us signals. Being in the passenger seat felt like the beginning of an adventure.

The ride had its own kind of music. The hum of the V8 beneath us, the tires whispering over asphalt, the endless ribbon of road unfurling straight into the mirage ahead. I'd press my forehead to the glass, breath fogging the window, eyes wide as wheat fields and windmills slid by in orderly rows. The silence between us wasn't heavy; it was ceremonial. Daddy's quiet carried weight, as if words might disturb the importance of the journey. He sipped from his silver thermos, exhaling softly after each drink, and I matched my breaths to his—learning steadiness without a single lesson spoken.

And then came the turn off the highway. The dirt road rattled us, dust trailing behind like an entourage. My stomach flipped with anticipation, because I knew what waited at the end: the derrick rising thin and sharp against the blue, a crown marking the kingdom of oil. The air shifted—metal, earth, diesel—an aroma I associated not with labor but with belonging.

The men were already watching for us. By the time Daddy eased to a stop, I was sitting tall, ready for my entrance. I jumped down in my little coveralls and saddle shoes, ponytail swinging, and the crew clapped and whistled as though the show had begun. I knew their hands were rough, their faces carved by sun, but to me they were an audience, and I was the belle of the ball. I grinned big, cheeks hot with pride, pretending their attention was routine.

They teased me, showing off doughnuts gone stale and bottles of Coke sweating in the shade, offering treasures as if they were gifts for a visiting princess. One draped a rattlesnake over barbed wire like a trophy. Another rattled a dried tail in his palm, the sound sharp and thrilling. I squealed, delighted and utterly fearless. They laughed as if I were the spark that brightened the whole rig.

There was a forbidden door: the doghouse, with its dim light and walls plastered with pinup girls. Daddy said it was no place for me. But sometimes, when the machinery stilled, JC crooked a sunburned finger and ushered me in. The haze of cigar smoke swirled above his head, and the faded smiles on the walls looked secret and dangerous. I giggled, sensing I was in on something I shouldn't be. JC's laugh thundered back, and for that instant I felt like his co-conspirator, trusted in a way no one else was.

Outside again, the rig clattered and groaned, tools striking metal like percussion, the derrick dipping and lifting in a steady dance. I wandered the site with the confidence of someone who knew she was adored. This was Daddy's world, but when I was there, it felt like it was mine too.

The grand finale was always the malt shop on the way home. A bent tin sign promised BURGERS & SHAKES, and stepping inside was like stepping into color after black-and-white. Neon buzzed overhead, fry baskets hissed in hot oil, and the sweet churn of the shake machine filled the air. Daddy ordered me a hamburger—meat and mayonnaise only—and those curly fries, one long golden ribbon I pulled apart slowly, savoring the crisp edges and soft insides.

Milkshakes were required—vanilla for me, chocolate for him. And then came the secret coda, his smile tugging at the corner of his mouth as he bent down to whisper, "If you promise not to spill, I'll get a soft serve for the road."

Blue leather or not, I always promised. And I always dripped. Ice cream down my coveralls, pooling in the curve of my saddle shoes. He'd pull over, laughing, mopping me up with napkins, his eyes crinkling with something I rarely saw at home—delight.

The ride back was slower, golden light slanting across the fields. Windows down, the wind whipped through my hair, carrying dust, hay, and a trace of diesel. I curled against the door, lulled by the hum of the engine, eyelids heavy. Somewhere between pump-jacks and town, I'd wake to see him glance over at me, and there it was—that private smile, small but undeniable, as if to say, *This day was ours.*

And it was. Those rides were pure glory, a world apart from the everyday, a stage where I could shine without fear. At home, words often went unspoken, silences stretched, and I sometimes wondered if I'd ever been fully seen. But in the Lincoln, with dust in the air and oil fields stretching wide, I was seen.

What I didn't know then was how much I would chase that feeling later in life—the sense of being chosen, singled out, worth the effort of the drive. It became the measure by which I weighed love: whether someone would glance over in the golden light and smile just for me.

Even now, when I catch the flash of chrome in sunlight or smell diesel on the wind, I'm back there—his chosen passenger, belle of the oil patch ball, certain the entire sky belonged to us. And maybe that is what I have been reaching for ever since: the promise tucked into that glance, the unspoken assurance that, for one stretch of dusty road, I mattered.

CHAPTER 26:

SAYING GOODBYE TO MY DADDY

BONES BENEATH THE PRAIRIE
ROSEANN MAYER

PART 1: THE LAST VISIT

D addy's last visit came quietly, like a reckoning.
It had the stillness of those long drives we once took together—steady, unhurried, with the unshakable sense that something waited at the end.

A few weeks before he died, he drove to Houston alone—not with his wife, Jane. He said he needed to speak with me "face to face." The children were at school. My ex was gone. The house held a heavy silence that comes before a storm.

I remember the sound of his briefcase latch snapping open. He paused before lifting the lid. His hands—usually precise—trembled slightly. Not from age. Not from anger. But from something harder to bear: resolve.

He knew everything.

The business he had bought for me—his legacy, his faith in me—was crumbling. He'd found forged credit cards. Legal documents with his name he'd never signed. Unauthorized loans. He didn't need a forensic accountant. His instincts had already done the work: two sets of books, missing commissions, a paper trail of betrayal.

He had trusted the wrong man.

The living room smelled faintly of our wet Irish setter and stale coffee. Afternoon light came in through the blinds, turning dust into slow snow. He pulled a stack of papers from the case and set them on the coffee table, aligning the corners like it mattered that one thing, at least, be square. He didn't look at me right away. He read the top page as if confirming a verse from memory, then placed it face up so I could see the dates.

The dates told the truth.

Then he handed me the papers—signed, notarized, final. He was giving me the company outright. Every share. Every obligation.

"I want no part of what I believe is about to happen," he said. His voice was firm but not cruel. "You handle it. See if you can fix it."

I sat frozen, the documents stiff in my hands. It wasn't punishment. It was a charge. And a chance to do right—if I was strong enough.

He didn't hug me, not then. That wasn't our language. But he stayed a minute longer than he needed to, studying my face the way he used to read horizons—gauging weather, looking for wind. I nodded once to show I understood. It was one of the few times in my life I spoke his language fluently: spare words, long promises.

That afternoon, he told me what he planned to do.

"I'm going to the office," he said, his voice flat as a ledger line. "I'm going to tell him I've turned the company over to you. Every share. Every obligation. He'll hear it from me."

Hours later, Daddy told me how my ex had acted blindsided, wide-eyed, as though hearing for the first time about forged credit cards, false documents, missing funds. He swore he did not know. Said it must have been me. Claimed he'd been trying to clean up my mess.

Daddy didn't argue. He didn't raise his voice. He simply left, got in his car, and drove back to West Texas alone. The message was obvious—he'd handed the reins to me, and whatever came next had my name on it.

That night, when my ex came home, he already knew there would be questions. He dropped his keys on the counter like nothing had happened, tossed out a few explanations, a few excuses, and the same thin smile he used when he thought charm could outpace truth. "It's yours now," he said finally. "So why keep going on about it?" He let the word hysterical hang between us without saying it.

But I wanted the truth, and I wasn't letting go. I pressed harder, my voice low but steady, treading on thin ice with every challenge to his integrity. I knew the danger in that—the way the air changed when he felt cornered—but I couldn't stop. Deep down, I already knew there was no safe way back from the answers I was asking for.

A few days after that last hard conversation, Daddy called to tell me he'd been scheduled for bypass surgery. He said it plainly, like reading a grocery list. I asked whether he wanted me to come.

"Nah," he said. "A bunch of my friends have had it done. Nothing to it."

He meant it. But something in me—small and steady—said otherwise. A nudge in the heart I couldn't explain. We had been closer since he married Jane, or at least it felt that way. The edges between us had softened, the air easier to breathe.

The day before surgery, I rose before dawn and headed west, the September light spilling across the highway in ribbons of gold. The miles stretched out like an old hymn, steady and familiar. By evening, I was in his and Jane's living room, the three of us visiting about nothing in particular—neighbors, weather, the small things that keep a night easy. I kept it light, careful not to stir the air with business. His little brown bottle of nitro sat on the table between us, a silent reminder of why I'd come.

That night I slept in their guest room, the house breathing quietly around me. And in the morning, we dressed in half-light, moving without hurry. Together we drove to the hospital, the car filled with both routine and weight. The day had already decided what it would be.

The hospital was chill air and fluorescent mercy. Machines beeped at their altars, nurses moving like practiced choir members. In pre-op, he lay propped on white pillows, his hair thinned to silver threads, his skin mapped with bruises, tape, and the faint trace of iodine at his sternum. I watched the pulse in his neck, steady but tired. He looked smaller than I remembered, and more himself than ever.

Jane, my sister Louise, and I were all there. We made polite small talk with the anesthesiologist. We laughed at nothing because that's what people do when terror is in the room and no one dares name it. Louise straightened his blanket three times. Jane smoothed the sheet as if tucking in a story.

He asked about the children. About school schedules, a choir recital he would miss, whether the oldest was still playing ball. He nodded as if keeping books in his head—debits, credits, what was owed. He told Jane he wanted fried chicken when it was all over. "Real fried chicken," he said, and the nurse smiled like she'd heard that one before.

As they wheeled him toward surgery, I lingered behind. The hallway seemed too long, the doors too wide for such a narrow body. The air smelled of bleach and boiled linen.

I reached for his hand—a first for me. A small gesture, but sacred. "I love you," I said.

He looked me straight in the eye. "I love you too."

It was the only time I ever heard those words from him. And I never heard them again.

I stood still long after the doors closed, looking at my hand as if it had caught a bird that might fly away if I breathed too loud. Jane touched my shoulder once and let it rest there. She didn't fill the silence. Kindness can be so quiet.

While he was in the OR, I found the chapel—one of those small, all-faith spaces with a single stained-glass window that didn't offer to be art, only light. I sat on the back pew and folded in on myself. I didn't pray with words. I prayed with bated breath. Let him live. Or let him go easy. And let me do what's mine to do.

&

The surgeon came out later with the voice surgeons use—professional comfort, chart words softened for daughters. He'd be in ICU overnight. The timeline marched forward like a metronome no one could stop.

&

That evening—while he lay sedated in ICU—my cell phone rang. I walked to the lobby to answer.

It was my ex.

Another crisis. Perfectly timed. The IRS was coming tomorrow to seize the business 450 miles away.

His tone was brisk, almost bemused, as if this were just more paperwork in a life made of paperwork. He talked too fast, piling facts into a wall I couldn't climb: revenue officers, padlocks, inventory control, assets soon to wear government stickers.

No husband. No children. No one to shield me. Just me in a hospital hallway, surrounded by death and debt, grief and God. And once again, I was the one to carry it.

Part Two: My Dad's Good Name

I don't even remember the drive back to the house—only the panic that rose from deep in my chest and locked my throat. My hands shook so badly I couldn't dial the lawyer's number straight. My vision blurred—not only with tears, but with fury and fear. Shame pressed down like a stone.

Because once again, I had carried disaster to someone else's door.

Jane's face said everything—disbelief, sorrow, fury. And she had every right. This was supposed to be her goodbye—her moment with the man who had given her love again after nearly fifty years of marriage to someone else. She had walked her own long road of loss and starting over. Those last days should have been filled with nothing but quiet mornings, hand-holding, and the grace of shared memories. Instead, I had brought ruin. Not by choice. By consequence.

And still—she didn't yell. She didn't scold. She just looked at me, heartbroken.

That silence hurt more than anything.

By the second day of Daddy's hospital stay, the reality could no longer wait. The business could not survive without protection. Chapter 11. Not a clean slate, but a pause, a chance to breathe.

I filed over the phone from the hospital waiting room, my voice low, explaining to the Houston lawyer while machines hummed in the background and the coffee in my cup went cold. A courier arrived with papers that had to be signed immediately. Because my ex was still treasurer of the corporation, his signature was required too. I scrawled my name on page after page, then sent the packet back the same way it had come.

By the fourth day, the doctors told us it was close. Many of Daddy's friends had gathered in the room—men and women who had known him for decades. We stood in a soft circle around his bed, hands linked, voices low. Someone began a hymn. Others joined in. We prayed. We sang. We wept.

It was a comfort I hadn't expected, to be surrounded by that kind of love.

He had been on the ventilator for three days by then; the medication pulling him far away. By the first morning of that third day, he was already drifting in and out of a heavy coma. We never got to speak again.

When the end came, it was quiet. His chest rose and fell in a slowing rhythm until it didn't anymore, and the room seemed to exhale with him.

৯

That night, back at Jane's house, grief lay heavy in the rooms. She pulled my sister and me aside, her eyes steady.

"I want him buried beside your mother," she said.

They had only been married eighteen months. But she understood. And it was a mercy I hadn't known I needed.

৯

We planned another grand funeral—another cathedral of grief. Hundreds of people came. Episcopal liturgy in a Baptist church, huge and old and beautiful, the sanctuary that seemed to hold its breath for the occasion. Scripture, flowers, suits in the pews. A man of quiet strength laid to rest with all the honor he deserved.

Before the service, Jane—God bless her—pulled my sister and me aside.

"I want him buried beside your mother," she said. "That would be the greatest blessing to us all."

They had only been married eighteen months. But she understood. And it was a mercy I hadn't known I needed.

I stood by his grave with debt on my shoulders and West Texas dust clinging to my shoes. We were in Albany—the same Beehive lunch, the same voices rising together to sing "Prairie Land," the Fandangle anthem, before they lowered him down. The rope creaked as it took his weight for the last time. I wept.

And as I wept, another truth hollowed me out: with Daddy gone, my last lifeline was cut. He had been my shield in ways I hadn't admitted—not just financial, but the steady presence I could lean against, the knowledge that if I truly broke, someone strong would catch me. Now there was no one. No money to rescue me. No father to steady me. Just me, raw and exposed, tethered to a man I no longer trusted, with children I had to protect and debts I couldn't outrun. The grief wasn't only for him; it was for the terrifying question that rose like wind in my bones: How on earth would I survive without him?

My husband stood beside me, solemn but unflinching, his shadow brushing mine on the baked grass. Even in my grief, I pictured a world where he never drew another breath beside me. The scent of funeral flowers clung to us both, and the heat pressed down, but it wasn't the sun that burned—it was knowing that from this day forward, I could not stand the sight of him. Something in me ended there at the graveside. Not on my feet yet, but in my head, the door had already shut.

Ahead lay the reading of my father's will, the truth waiting like a stone in the road I could not swerve around. And after that—seven days later—Houston. The lawyer's office would carry the stale scent of paper and coffee gone cold, the blinds drawn against a sun I wouldn't care to see. My husband would sit beside me, Treasurer's title still stitched to his name, close enough for his heat to reach me but never his hand.

Between us, a stack of documents as thick as a family Bible. Debtor in Possession glared from the top of each page like an accusation.

I would take the pen, my hand moving in mechanical loops, the black ink eating my name until it was no longer mine. Somewhere between one page and the next, a switch would flip. I would know. I would be done. I would carve my way free, reclaim my maiden name, scrub clean the stain of his dirty, shameful, con name. In my mind, I would already be gone, the marriage a husk I had stepped out of. That moment would sear itself into me, sharp and exact, as if I could still feel the paper beneath my hand even decades later.

And in that paper-shuffling quiet, the air heavy with endings, I would hear it—the rope's slow, steady creak—only now it was my life with him being lowered away, one page at a time.

CHAPTER 27:

THE WILL AND THE DEBT

BONES BENEATH THE PRAIRIE
Roseann Mayer

The slow creak of the rope lowering Daddy into the earth hadn't yet left my ears when the next act began. Flowers wilted in sunlit pews, their perfume turning heavy in the heat. Casserole dishes sent back with crumbs under their foil (and I knew better, I just didn't have the will to clean them); thank-you notes lay half-written in my purse. The grief was still raw, unabsorbed, when the next blow landed.

It started with the will.

We gathered—just Jane, Louise, and me—around a polished mahogany table. The leather chairs gave an inaudible sigh as we sat. Stripes of sunlight cut across the rug, as though even the day knew to tread lightly. The air had a tight, unnatural quiet that made you conscious of every breath, every shift in your seat.

Daddy had been careful. Jane would have life insurance to sustain her. The rest of the residuary estate—what was left after the debts and bequests—would be divided equally between Louise and me, with provisions for our children.

I was stunned. My mother had told me two years earlier I'd been cut out entirely, that she'd made her wishes clear. And I believed her.

But in the end, my father hadn't followed her instructions. He'd left us equal on paper. That knowledge softened something in me—it didn't erase her final words, but it dulled the sting. For a moment, I could believe he still saw me.

But the genuine power didn't lie in the numbers. Daddy had named Louise sole executrix of the estate and trustee of the Generation-Skipping Trust. She alone would control when and how anything moved, and to whom.

She took her place at the head of the table as if it had always been hers. Arms folded. Chin high. She didn't look at me once.

I told myself grief might bridge the gap—that we could meet somewhere in the middle, sisters carrying the burden together. But I didn't yet understand that the erasure had already begun. The rivalry between us was over. And she had won.

The finality hit harder than the words themselves: with Daddy gone, I had lost my lifeline. His presence had been both shield and anchor—physical protection, financial backing, the quiet strength that steadied me when everything else swayed. Without him, I felt exposed, like someone had cut the last rope between me and the shore. Vulnerability settled into my bones. How on earth could I survive without him?

꘎

Not long after I left West Texas, I walked straight into another eruption—this one in my home.

My future ex-husband and I sat across from our bankruptcy attorney, an old friend of mine. His office smelled faintly of leather and paper, lined with shelves of law books. He knew about the trust, the debt, the maze I'd been trying to navigate.

At one point, he leaned back and said, "I've never in my life seen a trust written with such control from the grave."

We were there for the Chapter 11 bankruptcy meeting for Creative Cabinets.

The number hit me like a punch—$250,000 in unpaid payroll taxes. I knew what a 941 was; I'd heard my husband rail about it for years. But I thought it was handled. I believed the bookkeeper filed the reports, and he signed the checks.

He had fired the bookkeeper; he told me he'd handled it himself—that the payments had been made. I never saw the checks. I believed him anyway. My role was in sales and promotion. The books were never mine to touch. Daddy had tried, but even he only saw what my husband allowed him to see.

Now, sitting across from the lawyer, I watched as my husband leaned forward, voice low and measured, and said it was all a mistake. The IRS had lost the checks. He hadn't realized they'd never been cashed. He sighed, shook his head, and let the weight of imagined incompetence settle in the room like dust.

For a moment, watching him, I remembered the man who once charmed entire rooms with that same calm, who could talk his way into opportunities no one else could touch. That gift—misapplied as it was now—had once made me feel like we might survive anything.

I felt my jaw tighten, my hands curling around the edge of the chair until the leather bit into my palms. I knew this performance—this calm, put-upon reasonableness. I also knew it was a lie. But I stayed silent, tasting the metallic edge of restraint.

He would deny the truth until the day we divorced.

Then came the moment that split time in two.

"We need to rewrite the ownership documents," my husband said smoothly. "I'm a working partner. Her father always meant for me to own half."

I stared at him. Then at my lawyer. Waiting for someone to stop it.

The lawyer's pen hovered. "Let's hold on to that for now," he said. Later in the hall, he whispered, "This isn't the time to fight him. We'll protect your rights—but not today."

What my husband was doing wasn't careless. It was calculated. He knew how to look reasonable in a room like that—how to lower his voice, slide the pen forward as if burdened by work instead of deception.

Back home, without my asking, he justified it in the language he knew best—religion. We were partners; he said. He was already doing more than half the work. Keeping it divided wasn't Scriptural. And then, with a look that made my stomach turn, he lorded it over me like the sword of Damocles.

In the months ahead, I would find myself caught between two storms—my future ex-husband on one side, my sister on the other. And with no parents left to help me navigate, I would have to face them both on my own, with no net beneath me. In those months, I would miss the one voice that had always steadied me.

❧ Interlude—A Father's Voice

Months after he passed, I stumbled on the old voicemail—just one of his regular check-ins, the kind he left without fuss. He was asking about the baby, about the heat, and reminding me to rotate my tires. "You always forget," he chuckled. "I hope you're well. Maybe I'll see you next month."

I must have played it a hundred times—not because I needed the reminder, but because hearing it made me feel like he was still just a call away. Like he might pick up if I dialed. Say my name the way only he could. I needed that voice more than I could admit.

There was so much I wanted to tell him—about the bankruptcy, the betrayal, the way the ground had shifted until I didn't know which direction was forward. I wanted to tell him how ashamed I was—how it all felt too big for me. But the silence on the other end was real now. Immovable.

So, I went back to the picture of him I knew best: seated at the kitchen table in his robe, a half-drunk cup of coffee beside the *Wall Street Journal*, the local paper folded underneath, and the *New York Times* crossword already half-filled before the rest of us had even poured milk in our cereal. He would grumble at headlines, circle things in ink, tap his pencil against the table like a slow metronome of thought. A rhythm I took for granted then, but can still hear now.

He told me once—his voice low, his tone unbending: "You show up. You gut up. You get it done. Because that's what's expected. And because you grew up making things right. That's how we do it."

He didn't offer comfort. He offered expectation. Steadiness. He trusted I could carry the load, even when I didn't.

And I did. Even when I wanted to crumble, I got up. I dressed the baby, called the bank, and sat through meetings with lawyers, stringing the pieces of my life back together with the quiet resolve he had always expected of me. I showed up because that's what he taught me to do—not to wait for a rescue, but to hold the line, no matter how frayed it got.

One afternoon, I found an old postcard tucked into a forgotten drawer—Greece, faded blue sky and crumbling columns, a quick note scrawled in his neat hand: *We stood here minutes ago, your mother and I. She says you would love the olives.*

Her name was there too, curling beside his like it always had—just as she used to sign birthday cards in her delicate script, the ink looping as if it were dancing. It must've been the last trip they took before she got sick.

I held that card for a long time, tracing the edges, imagining them there—tanned, smiling, unburdened by the years that would follow. I didn't need the postcard, not really. But holding it grounded me. It reminded me there had been joy once. And that he had wanted to share it with me.

Some fathers leave behind money or land—tangible things you can inventory or split. Mine left those too. But more than anything, he left a backbone: a quiet, steady strength threaded through everything I do. A way of moving through the world with intention. A belief in showing up, even when the room is cold, even when the odds are long.

And now, when I feel myself slipping—when that old voice says you are not enough—I hear his instead. Not soft or lyrical, but clear and sure: Gut up. Get it done.

I still pick up the phone sometimes, still catch myself halfway through dialing. Of course, there's no answer. Not in the way there once was.

But sometimes, in the quiet, I feel the echo—a breath at my back, a presence just out of view. And that's enough.

His love was never wrapped in flourishes. It was built into the structure of things—into the expectation that I could handle what came.

That I would.

That I did.

And that I still do.

I carry his steadiness in my bones, his dignity in my bearing. When I married my second husband, I was proud to take his name, and yet when I signed it for the first time, I knew I was also carrying my father's—woven quiet and sure beneath the ink. His good name was never just letters. It was a way of standing in the world, and I stand there still.

Until the day I couldn't hear his voice anymore.

CHAPTER 28:

NO NET BELOW ME

BONES BENEATH THE PRAIRIE
ROSEANN MAYER

After my father died, the world tilted.

There was no steady voice to call, no one behind a closed door who would tell me the truth and mean it. The quiet was deafening—not just in the house, but in my life. I still had my children. I still had my faith—thank God for that—but everything else felt like it had been yanked away in an instant. The scaffolding of my world had collapsed.

For a time, I told myself I wasn't truly alone. My portion of the Generational Trust Daddy had left—the one meant to protect me— was still there. Or so I thought. Louise held it tight, like pearls clutched to her chest—a weapon she seemed to wield not just from spite, but from something older. We'd fought each other since we could walk, two little girls acting out a war we didn't start.

Maybe she believed she was doing what Daddy wanted. He'd told her I'd spend it all in a year. And to be fair, I'd given him reason to think so. I'd always stretched beyond my means, chasing something I couldn't name. He put her in charge to preserve what little remained, for my sake and for my children. That was the logic. Maybe she thought she was protecting me from myself, carrying out his last instructions. But to me, it wasn't just money she withheld. It was mercy.

The trust became another lock I couldn't pick. No cushion. No rope. No net below me.

With my father gone, all illusions of safety vanished. I was a mother of three in a marriage that had turned into a war zone. I knew the next outburst could be the one I didn't get up from, and that his rage could spill over onto the kids. I wore the mask and played my part in public, even as fear became part of my bones.

I turned to the only thing I had left: my faith. I prayed in parking lots, in the bathroom at church, in the kitchen after the house went still. Once, I knelt beside the dryer with a towel in my mouth so the kids wouldn't hear me cry. The drum was still warm from a finished load, static clinging to my clothes, the sweet scent of fabric softener heavy in the air. The steady hum of the motor covered what I couldn't let escape. I prayed for joy—not peace, not love, but joy—because it was the only weapon I had against despair.

Verses went on sticky notes in the pantry. I whispered Scripture while folding laundry. Kept a tiny cross in my pocket that I worked until my knuckles ached. Anything to remind me there was still light.

What I wanted was the truth. Not the courtroom kind, not the Sunday-morning kind, but the kind you cling to just to stay sane. I'd lived too long with a man who twisted facts to fit his mood. One day we were flush; the next, broke. One day faithful; the next, gone. If I questioned him, I was mocked or accused of being unstable.

Over time, he convinced me I couldn't trust my mind—that I was too dramatic, too broken to be believed. The lies ran so deep I wondered if maybe I was the problem.

It's a cruel way to live—when truth becomes a threat and silence feels safer.

I didn't want wealth or comfort. I wanted a life where I could speak without being punished. Where my children could ask questions without fear. Where I could breathe without apology.

I prayed for that. In the carpool line. Over dishes. In the still hours of the night.

Give me a life of truth. Whatever it costs.

And in the cracks between exhaustion and fear, a small spark appeared.

Albany.

Not as a plan, but as a feeling—soft at first, like a half-remembered lullaby. It wasn't escape I pictured, but return. Not freedom, but home. I saw folding chairs under mesquite trees. A courthouse clock ticking. A porch swing in the evening light. A place where my name meant more than the bruise.

It wasn't a strategy yet, but it kept me breathing.

And in that breath, in the hush between sleep and waking, I heard it:

Then you'll have to walk through fire to get it.

And I knew I would.

If truth meant fire, I would walk through it.

No net below me. Only fire ahead.

And one night, the fire came knocking—loud enough to wake the children, sharp enough to split the life I had been clinging to. It was the beginning of the end.

CHAPTER 29:

THE BEGINNING OF THE END

❖

BONES BENEATH THE PRAIRIE
Roseann Mayer

The floor of the closet had long since given way beneath me, the carpet pressed flat from restless pacing. Barefoot, legs folded tight, I sank into the small square of darkness as if it could hide me. The air smelled of dust and cedar. The silence was thick enough to hear the house breathe. A cordless phone rested heavy in my lap. It was the late 1990s, when phones still felt solid, when you could believe they carried more than voices—bad news, maybe, or if you were blessed, a sliver of truth.

I'd prayed for truth, and when it came, it came like fire.

The voice on the other end belonged to Eileen. My prayer sister, hundreds of miles away. A bond forged not in chatter or gossip but in silence, in scripture whispered over each other's lives, in petitions that sometimes felt like lifelines. She and her husband had known mine. They liked him, admired him even, believed him to be steady, trustworthy. They could never have imagined the things I said out loud that day.

Words tumbled out, jagged and uneven, but not without hesitation. To soften the blow—for her, and perhaps for me—I reminded her of the better version of him. How he could be generous, how he worked hard, how once, long ago, he had prayed over me in the middle of the night when fear kept me from sleep. That man had felt real once. I wanted her to remember him, because I wanted to believe he was still in there, buried beneath the ruin. But even as I said it, I knew I was bending the truth, straining to hold on to a version that might have saved us.

The fire of honesty burned hotter. He was having another affair. This one was reckless enough to destroy not just a marriage, but a life. Company funds—our company's money—bled out into hotels, weekend trips, fine dinners meant for payroll and rent. The passwords were locked. The reports had stopped. Every question I asked met a wall.

Confronting him would not bring another bruise. It would be worse. His temper had shifted to something darker, colder. The fear inside me no longer belonged to me alone; it coiled around my children like a second skin.

Nights became vigils. Sitting on the stairs, I strained for the sound of his truck pulling into the drive, the slam of the door, the measured footsteps across the tile. Every prayer was the same: don't let the children come find me sitting there, waiting.

When the silence broke with Eileen's voice, it cut clean. I pictured her hand covering her mouth, Bible splayed beside her, breath steadying before she said it.

"Get out of there! Go to a shelter. Now. This is not God."

The word shelter fell like a stone into deep water, the ripples reaching everything I thought I knew about my life. At forty-six, with three children, a business, and a name that carried weight in the community, I was being told to run. I wore tailored suits, kept my place on the same church pew every Sunday, hosted dinners behind polished doors. No one knew what happened inside them.

The stone sank. *Shelter.* Not shame. Not pride. *Shelter.* Certainty. If I stayed, I might die.

Tears came in a rush, not from weakness, but from recognition. I believed her. Because I knew him. Leaving would mean he burned everything behind me, and I'd seen the fire before: lies already spreading, records withheld, money vanished as if it had never existed. I'd watched him erase child support from his first marriage, forge tax returns, twist the truth until it bent into whatever shape he needed.

Images rose like smoke: the steak knife landing inches from my hand, his laugh sharp and casual afterward; a shattered frame on the floor; sleeves tugged down to hide angry red marks; the wide, silent eyes of my children, watching.

This is not love.

From the ashes of fear, anger stirred—quiet, defiant: You don't have to live like this.

The thought was dangerous, but it became oxygen. I imagined leaving—not in a burst of flight, but step by deliberate step. Making copies. Calling shelters under false names. Opening a separate account. Breathing again. Wondering what memories my children would carry if I stayed and never got out.

Sleep didn't come that night. The closet held me until sunrise. At three in the morning, I heard him return, the bathroom faucet running, the low drone of the TV. I stayed still.

Dawn light brought resolve. Eileen remained at my side—quiet, fierce, unshakable. She prayed out loud when I couldn't find words, made calls when I was afraid to, reminded me I wasn't crazy.

As I was showering, with steam rising like incense, I whispered into the tile: God, if you want me to go, make it so clear I cannot ignore it.

Three days later, he came home from what he said was a business trip—cabinetry for a wealthy oilman's wife in East Texas. Plausible. Always plausible. He always had new clients.

But the details betrayed him. A collar rumpled, khakis that smelled faintly of perfume I didn't wear. Sunburn edged across his neck—the kind earned beside a pool, not in a workshop. Sand clung stubbornly to the cuffs of his pants. He dropped his bag in the hallway like a man who wanted to be caught.

His story was casual. His eyes refused mine.

And I knew.

It was a dare. The end had begun, even if no papers had yet been signed.

Something in me shifted that moment. I was no longer begging for love. I was listening for the exit.

When it came, I would take it.

Because survival isn't always loud or heroic. Sometimes it's quiet. Hidden. Drenched in fear. But survival all the same.

And I intended to survive.

Sometimes survival means seizing a way out the moment it appears.

… I had no net below me. Only fire ahead. And at last, I was ready to walk through it.

§❧

I had twenty-two years to walk away, and I didn't. You may wonder why. Some will say I was a fool, and sometimes I've said the same to myself. But this is how the trap was built: he convinced me the business would fail without him, that I couldn't run it alone. I had no real savings, no safety net to start over with three children. He promised I'd get no support, no share of what I had poured myself into, no help from anyone. And he said it often enough that I believed him. Add to that the vows I carried, the church that praised endurance, the fear of what he might do if I pushed too hard—and staying became its own form of survival. From the outside it looks like cowardice; from the inside it felt like the only way to keep a roof over my children's heads.

So when the chance came, I reached not for freedom but for detour. I told myself the lake house might save me—give me space to think, to breathe, to believe life could be different. And for a moment it almost did. But he always had a key. He would appear without warning, lean in the doorway, and say, "I told you I was coming." The lock meant nothing. Even there, I was never safe.

The lake house wasn't escape. It was a fragile rehearsal, a glimpse of what it might mean to belong to myself again. It didn't free me, but it reminded me I was still someone worth saving. And that reminder carried me toward the fire I would finally walk through.

But survival doesn't always arrive in the form you expect. Sometimes it comes dressed as detours—choices that look like freedom but are only another kind of cage. Before I walked through the fire, I reached for beauty. I reached for escape. I reached for a house on the lake.

❧ INTERLUDE—THE LAKE HOUSE ESCAPE

In 1999, a slight distribution from my inheritance came through via a check—part of the trust my father had set up. Not a fortune, but enough to plant roots somewhere different. Somewhere quieter. This is how I remember it: the choices I made, the way the lake felt to me in those years, both in sunlight and in the quiet that came after. I could have used that money to leave. I could have vanished into the night, taken the kids, and started a new life. But I didn't. Not then.

We always lived beyond our means, and that is mine to own. Overspending was my flaw, my greatest weakness. I treated it like a salve, as if a new dress, another set of dishes, or even a lake house could soften what felt unbearable inside. He didn't drive that; I did. The lake house wasn't just a dream for the kids or for us as a family—it was my way of buying a little hope, a place where I could believe, if only on weekends, that life was beautiful again.

So we bought the lake house. It wasn't a grand estate, but it sat on a gentle slope above the water, framed by scrub oaks and dapples of gold light. The scent of cedar planks, the hum of a boat engine, the shimmer of sunlit water—it all called to me in a way that made the world feel wide open again. It reminded me of childhood summers—fish fries, screen doors, hot evenings humming with cicadas. I wanted that again. I wanted my children to know it too.

Whatever else the lake house was for me, for the kids it was freedom—those weekends shimmered like the best kind of childhood, and I knew they'd carry those memories as joy, not survival.

Every Friday afternoon, I'd pack the SUV—three kids, their friends, the dog, coolers loaded with groceries, bags stuffed with swimsuits, towels, and snacks. By four o'clock, I was ready to hit the road. The kids didn't always leap in at the first call—teenagers had their own Friday night dreams—but more often than not; they came willingly, knowing that by sunset we'd be somewhere that felt like summer vacation.

The drive itself became ritualistic: AC on full blast, music spilling from the speakers, conversation bouncing between us about school, friends, and life. We laughed all the way there. I felt like a different version of myself—lighter, unhurried, in step with my children.

Most of the time, he came too, usually driving up later in his own truck after finishing work. Sometimes he surprised us with steaks for the grill or new tubes for the kids to tow behind the boat. He'd get the jet skis in the water, spend hours building the massive deck that wrapped around the house, or stand at the grill flipping burgers while the kids ran down to the dock. On those evenings, with smoke rising from the grill and laughter spilling across the yard, he almost looked like the man I'd once believed in. The kids adored those weekends with him—his presence felt bigger at the lake than it did at home, and for them, it really was one of the happiest times.

We had a sleek twenty-six-foot ski boat, polished to a shine, its hull reflecting the sky like liquid chrome. When we launched it, the engine roared to life, sending vibrations through the deck and laughter into the wind. The bow cut across the lake with ease, spray cool against sun-warmed skin. Fleetwood Mac, The Doobie Brothers, and Creedence made up our soundtrack. He liked to take the wheel, leaning back with an affable grin, proud of the way the boat carved across the water. And for those hours, when the sun caught his face and the children's hair streamed wild in the wind, I let myself believe we were ordinary.

On Saturdays, we'd be on the water at sunrise, gliding toward our favorite cove where families floated in clusters, tied together like a floating village. We'd throw anchor, and the kids would leap off the bow, chasing each other with squirt guns and sunblock-slick arms. The music played loud, the rhythm convincing me—if only for a while—that this was what life should feel like.

After a long day on and in the water, we'd run up the lawn to the deck, sunburned and sandy, muscles aching in the best way. Dinner was burgers or BBQ on the big front deck, string lights swaying in the evening breeze, the lake turning gold in the last light of day. We'd watch the sky fade to indigo, fireflies blinking on in the grass. On those nights, when he put his arm around me and pointed out constellations to the kids, I caught glimpses of the life I had once prayed for. It was fleeting, but real.

Sometimes, on warm nights when the moon scattered silver across the water, I'd sit alone on the dock, sweet tea in hand, the boards still warm beneath me. The cicadas hummed like distant drums, and the air wrapped around me like a prayer I hadn't yet spoken aloud. I'd think about the life I'd dreamed of—one where beauty didn't have to be earned by giving pieces of myself away—and wonder who I might have been if I'd believed that from the start.

Driving home on Sunday nights, I'd watch the shoreline fade in the rearview mirror and feel the quiet of the lake slipping away. The farther away we got, the more I knew how much I needed that place—not just for the water and the sun, but for the way it let me breathe.

It was only a couple of years after this that I left for good, but the lake had already begun teaching me what freedom could feel like.

Freedom doesn't come without a reckoning. The same fire that gave me glimpses of myself also gave me the courage to ask the questions I had once buried. And that was what lit the fuse.

CHAPTER 30:

PART 1: THE NIGHT OF NO RETURN

BONES BENEATH THE PRAIRIE
Roseann Mayer

I knew exactly what set him off that night. I pressed him about the phone calls to Alaska, the emails, the woman he claimed he was trying to "bring to Jesus." I demanded answers, and he hated I wouldn't let it go.

That was all it took.

Later, he'd say I pushed his buttons. That if I stayed quiet, didn't ask questions, didn't look at him the wrong way, everything would be fine. Somehow, it was always my fault. Always my doing.

His hand curled around the bedpost; polished mahogany gripped like a hammer. My heart leapt to my throat, ears ringing with blood. The air went still. All I heard was the creak of the floor beneath his feet and the jagged sound of my breath.

His face twisted into something unrecognizable—rage stripped of words. The moment thickened, slowed, like honey poured in winter. I saw his arm rise before I registered the weight behind it.

The bedpost whistled through the air before it struck—brutal and clean—against the meat of my thigh. The room tilted. I hit the ground hard, breath punched from my lungs. Lucy, my dog, growled frantically, circling, her nails scrambling against the floor. Pain bloomed fast, lightning under skin.

The bedroom was paneled in shadows, lit only by the flicker of a green marble fireplace. The four-poster loomed in the center, a relic from an older, crueler time.

The post dropped with a dull thud, clattering once against the hardwood before rolling, as if trying to flee.

From upstairs, I knew they could hear. The yelling. The crash. The kind of silence that follows a blow. What I had kept hidden behind closed doors had spilled into the open, seeping up the stairwell like smoke from a fire. My precious children—now they knew. They didn't just suspect anymore. They knew. What would they do with it? How would I ever explain?

Then something broke inside me—not fear, but fury. Not survival, but defiance. Fire surged hot in my chest. The line had been crossed.

This ends now.

I lunged. Clawed at his eyes, throat, any soft place I could reach. No longer shielding myself, I fought as if I meant it. A wildcat, yes—but fighting for my life.

Days earlier, I had confronted him about the financial inconsistencies. He had exploded. Then, without a word, pulled a loaded handgun from the dresser. Cocked it. Hurled it onto the bed between us.

"Shoot me if you have the guts," he snarled.

Everything went still. No yelling, no tears. Just the sickening weight of a weapon between us, silence too loud to bear.

I didn't move. Couldn't. My eyes locked on the gun. The air thickened, pressed. Time bent. For a heartbeat, I wasn't afraid—I was incandescent with fury. I wanted to return every ounce of pain he'd ever poured into me. To break him the way he had broken me.

But I didn't.

I stood trembling, scattered into emotional shards across that bed-spread. And I knew something had shifted for good. A gun on the bed is not a marriage. It is war.

And war always ends in surrender—or death.

&❧

That night, when the bedpost found my body, I was already standing at the cliff edge of decision. The yelling carried through the walls; a door opened upstairs and footsteps pressed against the landing. My children were junior high and high school aged then, and for eighteen years I had believed I'd managed to keep the darkest parts of our life hidden from them. But the sound of this—the crack of wood, the fury in his voice—could not be disguised. For the first time, the secret I had carried alone spilled into their world. The house itself bore witness, and so did they.

And with it came the shame that would cling to me for years—the bitter knowledge that I had sworn they would never know, and still I failed. Worse still, the very success of my silence became its own curse. Because I had hidden it so well, they grew up believing nothing was wrong. And now, when I speak the truth, they struggle to believe it. They see the life I worked so hard to make look normal—the birthday cakes, the soccer games, the family photos—and they can't reconcile it with the violence I buried beneath. What I thought was protection became a wall between us. My silence kept them safe for a time, but it also cost me their trust.

And it was in that moment I knew the reckoning had come — there would be no going back.

&❧

When the responders came, I was in damage control before the door even opened. Begged them not to arrest either of us. Lying. Saying it was mutual. "Nothing happened. We just argued. We're fine."

I covered bruises with sleeves. I swallowed blood into my mouth. I softened the story until it was unrecognizable.

They took him out to the garage to question him. I didn't know then that he showed them the scratches I'd left fighting for my life—arms, back, maybe chest—and told them I was the wildcat, the abuser, the danger. He said *I* was the crazy one.

And I almost believed it myself. That's the sickness of it.

I begged them not to believe him. Begged them not to press charges. It wasn't the first time responders had come—it was just the worst. Somehow, they left us both standing. The officers gave me a look that said, We'll be back. Next time, one of you won't be standing.

❧

When the taillights of their cruiser faded down the street, the silence in the house was unbearable.

I stood in the kitchen, leaning against the counter, my thigh throbbing where the post had struck. The clock ticked steadily, the refrigerator hummed, but the air itself felt cracked open. Upstairs, I could hear the faint shuffle of my children settling again into their rooms—quiet, too quiet. They had heard. They had seen. They would never forget.

And neither would I.

That was when I knew—really, finally knew—he might kill me. Not someday. Not metaphorically. Truly.

I decided to leave. Not later. Not when it was convenient. Not with a perfect plan. Just the raw instinct that if I stayed, I would not survive.

It wasn't brave—it was necessary. A flicker of clarity in the fog.

I looked at myself in the hallway mirror as I passed—hair tangled, lip split, eyes hollow but blazing. The woman staring back at me wasn't a victim anymore. She was someone on the verge of escape.

§❧

That night was the night of no return.

I had crossed a line inside myself, even if I hadn't yet walked out the door. There are moments you can't unlive, moments that break the story in half. That night was one of them.

For years, I had prayed for clarity—for God to tell me when it was time, for a sign so loud I couldn't ignore it.

The sign had come as wood against flesh, the sickening whistle of a bedpost swung in rage, the eyes of my children watching from the shadows, and the officers shaking their heads as they left me standing.

It had come, and I had heard it.

The end had begun.

§❧

Closing Note

The next day, I rose with a new resolve. Not the kind that looks like triumph, but the kind that looks like survival—quiet, determined, barely breathing.

I didn't yet know where I would go, or how. But I knew this much: I was leaving.

And once you know that, there is no going back.

CHAPTER 30:

PART TWO: THE LEAVING

❖◇❖

BONES BENEATH THE PRAIRIE
Roseann Mayer

The house was silent. Too silent. Every creak of the walls sounded like a warning.

He was gone for the weekend—off to the lake to fish, to drink, to disappear into whatever men like him do when no one's watching. Sleepovers and weekend plans had scattered the kids across the city, a blessed gift of distance. For the first time in months, I had the house to myself. I knew I might never get another chance.

The silence was thick, almost sacred, but edged with menace. I stood in it for a long moment, letting the quiet wrap around me like both a warning and a prayer. If a car pulled into the drive, if a neighbor saw me—everything would collapse.

In the days after our last fight, I moved like a ghost. A woman with a secret, going through the motions. I folded laundry like a machine, reheated food I didn't eat, set the dinner table for children who weren't home. Each gesture rehearsed, each step a lie. My breaths came shallow, clipped. I told myself they'd be safer if I left them. He didn't hurt them unless I was there to provoke him. I was always the excuse. That's the lie abused mothers tell themselves—the one that keeps us still until we can't stand still anymore.

They weren't little anymore—junior high and high school, nearly grown. Old enough to pack their own lunches, to drive soon, to carry secrets of their own. But they were still my children. Leaving them—even for one night—tore at something primal inside me. My body screamed against it, bone and blood refusing. I told myself that one day they'd understand. That one day they'd see the full picture. But no matter how old they got, they were still my babies. The ones I had rocked, nursed through fevers, whispered prayers over in the dark. Walking away felt like ripping a bone from flesh.

I didn't justify it. I couldn't. I just did what I had to do. And it broke me.

I didn't plan to be gone long. Just long enough to get clear. To find shelter. To breathe. Then I would come back for them. That was the vow running through my veins. I had the Trust, after all. Surely it could help me now. It was mine—my birthright, my security. But my sister hadn't let me near it in years.

When he left for the lake, I made my move.

&pause;

I swept through the house like a thief. Grabbing what mattered—clothes, folders, the office computer, the little wooden box of photos hidden under the guest bed. My hands shook so badly I dropped a stack of papers, crouched in panic, heart hammering like a drum.

I even pulled my parents' framed photo from the hallway wall, sliding it between sweaters as though their faces could guard me. I wasn't coming back. There would be no second sweep.

He controlled every cent. Even with my inheritance, someone always tied my hands. I yanked open the drawer where he hid things. Dug beneath old socks and crumpled receipts until my fingers hit it—plastic, cold, a credit card in my father's name. Years ago, he'd forged the application, mailed it to one of his secret PO boxes. I held it like a stolen key. Like a weapon. Anger boiled beneath my ribs. How many other lies had I mistaken for truths?

I had two hundred dollars in cash. That was all. I searched for hidden bills, secret stashes. Nothing. Just this card. One lifeline.

I loaded the SUV like a lifeboat—fast, frantic, breathless. The office computer went in first, then a box of photographs, folded clothes, my grandmother's quilt snatched from the closet as if it might catch fire if I hesitated. Every slam of a drawer reverberated through the house like a grenade. Every click of a lock cracked the silence like a bullet.

By the time the door shut behind me, the sound ricocheted across the driveway like a warning shot, and my hands shook on the wheel so violently I could hardly grip it. This was all I could carry forward. Everything else—our history, my safety, my dignity—I abandoned to him, left smoldering in the wreckage.

Upstairs, the laundry basket still waited. A small T-shirt sat on top, folded with care, the kind I had washed a thousand times, the fabric softened by years of soap and sun. Their voices weren't in the rooms, but they filled the air anyway, clung to the walls, pressed against my chest. Even in escape, I couldn't shake them. My children were ghosts in every doorway, watching, waiting, bearing silent witness. And I was leaving them behind in a house on fire.

The last thing I packed was Lucy. She sat at the top of the stairs, her head tilted, eyes fixed on me as if she already knew. My bulldog. Loyal. Steady. Untouched by his cruelty. I whispered her name, soft as a secret, and she came, silent but sure, her nails tapping the hardwood like a clock ticking down. I wrapped the leash around my wrist and held tight. She was my anchor, my second lifeline. She was coming with me.

❧

I stopped at a corner store on the edge of town, lungs burning with panic, my heart still galloping. I bought a pack of cigarettes—something I hadn't done in years, something he had forbidden, called trashy, beneath me. But tonight, it was defiance.

I stood in the sodium glow of the parking lot, tore one from the pack, lit it with shaking hands, and dragged in the smoke. It scalded my throat, bitter and raw. It was awful. It was freedom. Each exhale spiraled into the dark sky like rebellion rising, like a flare marking the line I had finally crossed. And it was mine, my choice.

§◦

I drove a few hours, sun glaring on the windshield, heat shimmering off the asphalt. Lucy pressed against my leg, her steady weight anchoring me. Smoke drifted out the cracked window, a ribbon of refusal unraveling into the bright, unyielding day.

My parents were gone. With them went the last true tether of safety I'd known. They had named Louise executrix of the family trust. She hadn't wanted me near it, or her, for years. She had always wanted control, and now she had it. She held the keys. I had nothing but bruises, a dog, and the frayed hope that blood might still mean something.

Though we hadn't spoken since Daddy's funeral, I drove to Louise's house. I believed she'd open the door. That she'd remember. That underneath the hardness, there might still be something soft.

It was evening by now. The porch light glared. Her car was in the driveway. TV flickered blue inside. I pulled Lucy close, climbed the steps like a woman walking into a church, half-prayer, half-confession.

The door opened part way. Her husband sat in the den, beyond earshot. For one suspended second, I let myself believe she'd throw it wide, wrap me in a blanket, make tea, whisper that she'd been waiting.

She didn't.

Her eyes were flat; her mouth thin. "What do you want?"

"He—he beat the crap out of me. With a mahogany bedpost. Slammed it into me—connected hard, more than once. The kids— they're not here, thank God—they're safe, just for now. He's at the lake, but he'll come back; he always does. If I don't get out—he's going to kill me. Please, I just need a place, a night or two, until I can find somewhere safe for all of us. Just a night or two. That's all."

Her gaze swept me once, cold as a verdict.

"You can't stay here," she said.

That was it. When Louise shut me out, it wasn't with argument or explanation—it was the flat slam of a door. I stood there dizzy, my stomach twisting so hard I thought I might be sick. My sister sealed me out like a stranger. The house behind her held the same air we'd breathed as girls, and yet I could not enter it.

I called George—my husband's best friend, a therapist, the last man on earth my husband would have wanted me to reach. In dialing his number, I crossed a line I could not uncross. A kind of betrayal, yes—but one born of desperation, of needing someone steady when every door around me was closing.

He answered.

No hesitation, no polite distance. His voice was sure, present, as if he had been waiting for the call all along. And in a night when so many doors had slammed shut, his voice felt like one opening.

I didn't cry. I didn't argue. I walked back to the car with no plan, no destination—only the need to disappear before the next blow landed.

I drove until neon cut through the dark and a flickering vacancy sign pulled me into an old roadside motel. The curtains gaped just enough to let the streetlight in; the air smelled of bleach and cigarettes and something hollow. The phone in my hand felt heavier than any suitcase I could carry.

We talked a little. His voice wrapped around me like cedar and soap—warmth that didn't demand, didn't bruise. It felt like betrayal and salvation, all tangled in one. Then the line went quiet, and I lay on the stiff bedspread as the phone lit up again and again—my husband's name flashing on the screen, hundreds of missed calls piling like stones. I didn't answer. I couldn't.

For two nights I stayed in that hollow room, listening to the buzz of the ice machine outside and letting silence throb in my chest. George checked in by phone, steady as the tide. On the third day he offered something more: a vacancy in an apartment complex near him, a place I could step into right away.

The next day, I signed the lease with a trembling hand. Paperwork that should have felt like freedom only felt like borrowed time. A day later, I was sitting in his living room, the curtains drawn, planning how to get my children out.

Something shifted. I was tired of being afraid. Tired of being touched only in anger. I wanted the safety he offered, yes—but I also wanted him, with a hunger that startled me as much as the fear I was fleeing.

I told him everything. The yelling. The bruises. The gun. I braced for doubt, for dismissal.

"You're not crazy," he said, elbows on his knees, voice low but certain. "You're in danger."

The first touch was both rescue and betrayal. I felt it scorch down my arms like fire. I had crossed a line I couldn't uncross—and I didn't care. My hand on his, his steady breath close to mine. Desperation made the choice for me. It was foolish; it was far from my beliefs; it wasn't wisdom. It was survival. And desire. To be wanted without being destroyed. To be seen and not erased.

But judgment came quickly, as I knew it would—whispers from church pews, sideways glances from neighbors, silence on the other end of the phone. *Why didn't you leave sooner? Why not while your parents were alive? Why not before your children could see?*

As if survival came with a calendar. As if timing could save a woman already drowning.

Abuse doesn't come with exit signs. It comes with silence—with slammed doors and locked accounts and nights where you wonder if the floorboards will give way under the weight of it. He didn't love me—he dismantled me. Took my body, my voice, the money my family gave us, and left me choking on shame.

I stayed. I thought staying made me strong. I thought leaving made me selfish.

George didn't see me as selfish. He saw me as alive. And when he knocked, I opened the door.

❧

When the sobs finally slowed, I lay in that bleach-scented motel bed—emptied, bruised, but breathing. Not whole. Not yet. But held, not harmed. I didn't know what would come next. But that night, I had warmth, breath, and someone who didn't flinch at my truth.

For the first time in years, I let go of the breath I'd been holding—the kind that lodges in the chest when you are always bracing for the blow.

And then, at last—I exhaled.

CHAPTER 31:

SCRATCHES ON THE GLASS

◆───◆◇◆───◆

BONES BENEATH THE PRAIRIE
ROSEANN MAYER

The day I rented the apartment, I stepped into the life I had already begun to stitch together. Bare walls, secondhand furniture—but mine. A thin thread of independence, a place where I could close the door and feel, for even an hour, that I belonged to myself again.

George lived across town, under the shade of pecan trees. His house was small but steady, clean and quiet in a way that felt like an answered prayer. I wasn't living with him at first. I had my own rented apartment—a front, a way to keep appearances—but I drifted more and more into his house, leaving the apartment behind except for show. It felt like a betrayal written in brick and mortar, yet it was also the only roof under which I could breathe. The house carried the illusion of normal life—meals on the table, laundry folded, lights glowing in the windows—but beneath it all was the truth I didn't want to face: I was still married, still breaking, still clinging to safety wherever I could find it.

I didn't turn to George because I loved him or because I saw a future; I turned to him because he was safe. In that moment, safe was everything. The romance—if you could even call it that—faded within a year, but the refuge he had offered, that window of air and quiet, kept me alive. I stayed nearly two years, piecing myself back together from the marriage I had barely survived.

And then the scratching started.

At first it was almost nothing: twigs snapping outside a window, the faint rustle of someone shifting just beyond the glass, a deliberate knock that made your breath hitch. A thin scrape against the screen, like a coin dragged across mesh. My chest would seize; my heart would pound so loud it erased the night. I would sit frozen in the dark, praying it would stop.

But it didn't.

One night a BB pellet cracked the outer pane of glass—ping—tiny starburst cracks running from a point the size of a pinhead. I wasn't there when it happened; the apartment was empty. Still, it was a message: not free, not safe. After that, I began to see him everywhere that mattered—a truck idling too long at a stoplight, a shadow in a stairwell, a figure in my rearview that looked unnervingly familiar. He haunted the edges of my days like a phantom with a grudge.

He escalated. He stole my truck next—slid in with a spare key and drove it off with his girlfriend riding shotgun. I had to drag him to court to get it back. He stopped paying rent on the commercial building still under my name, letting bills pile up on my shoulders like bricks until I was forced into legal fights no one seemed eager to care about. I brought records and receipts; I begged the courts to see what was obvious. They shrugged.

And he wasn't finished.

Everywhere I turned, his shadow stretched longer. He slipped inside my peace, my finances, my reputation. Whispers spread faster than the truth. I'd rebuild, only to find he'd poisoned the ground beneath me. I was no longer fighting for dignity—I was fighting for breath.

And then Lucy disappeared.

My bulldog. My steady shadow. One afternoon she was gone from George's backyard. No note. No trace. Just absence. Her collar still hung by the door. My throat closed tight; my knees buckled. I knew. Of course I knew. He had taken her. He couldn't have my body anymore, so he took what tethered me to myself.

For days I searched, calling her name down alleys, posting signs, checking shelters. Nothing. I drove in circles, stomach hollow, grief gnawing. I never found her. That wound never closed.

But something else did. The part of me that still excused him, still minimized, still whispered maybe he'll stop—that part died when Lucy vanished. Maybe I had failed once, maybe a thousand times, but not anymore. I was waking up.

&

By February 2000, my dear friend Rebecca had filed for divorce on my behalf. I didn't have the strength to navigate it alone, but she stood in the gap when I could not. What looked like failure was, in truth, God's mercy dragging me toward freedom.

He represented himself—cocky, contemptuous, every motion dripping with disdain. He missed deadlines, stonewalled requests, and laughed at orders. When my lawyer demanded business records, a box truck pulled up to her office and unloaded mountains of paper. Reams of blank printer sheets with the real financials scattered like landmines among them. No index, no folders. Just chaos.

It cost me dearly—time, money, dignity—to sift through that wreckage. But my lawyer was relentless, and eventually, we won. The house, the accounts, the business—everything but the husk of that commercial building, debt clinging to it like mold—were mine.

But even in victory, I felt no triumph. Just exhaustion.

Those who gaslight don't deal in truth. They deal in smoke and mirrors, erasing reality until you question your own pulse. God didn't make me a liar—I wasn't built to con or manipulate. All I wanted was the truth. And yet, the truth always seemed buried beneath layers of rumors, half-lies, and his honeyed rage.

Still, through the exhaustion, I longed for home.

The Albany of my childhood, not the one corrupted by whispers. White gloves. Kool-Aid in Miss Thelma's kitchen. My grandmother's robe, still faint with Estée Lauder. The prairie winds that smelled like cedar and rain.

I tried to build toward that dream. I found a freelance website design project—small, but mine, work I had earned with my own hands. It paid well enough. He was furious when he found out, called my client, and told him I was a substance abuser.

Let me say this clearly: I have never been a drug user. Not then. Not now. Not ever. I've smoked maybe two joints in my entire life. The strongest thing I ever took was a diet pill. Drugs were never my thing because I could not afford to lose control—I had already lived too much of my life with someone else controlling me.

So, when the pastor's question came— "Have you gotten clean?"—I felt the ground tilt. My stomach dropped. My mouth went dry. That's when I knew my ex's stories had grown legs. They had dressed themselves in Sunday clothes and taken a seat in the pews. My name had become a cautionary tale whispered in church hallways.

Only one part of it was true: I had run.

The rest were lies wrapped in scripture. Sanctified slander.

The calls kept coming—voicemails laced with venom, recycling rumors, inventing new ones. I was the scandal. The warning. The whisper.

But I didn't stop. I finished the project. I delivered the work. And in that small victory I found proof that I was not powerless, proof that no rumor—no matter how vicious—could erase the truth of what I built with my own hands.

I kept clawing my way back—not to innocence, not to perfection, but to myself.

I wasn't gone. I hadn't disappeared. I was still here. Still breathing. Still coming back.

One day, the scratches on the glass would fade into silence. One day, nothing would haunt me anymore.

And when that day comes, I would be more than a survivor. I would be a woman reborn.

CHAPTER 32:

THE BREAK-IN

◆

BONES BENEATH THE PRAIRIE
Roseann Mayer

A memory rises like steam at the edge of my vision.

It was 1962. Just up the road from our neighborhood stood a missile silo on the hill, Fritz the dog trotting ahead of me as if he belonged to the men in hard hats who worked there.

The silo wasn't a threat to me; it was a shield. Its silver skin caught the sun, shifting from white to gold to silver again, a kind of promise gleaming above our little town. The men who tended it seemed almost ceremonial in their movements—steady, watchful, guardians more than workers. Fritz loved them. They fed him scraps from their sandwiches, scratched his ears while my mother's skirt whipped in the caliche dust as she called him back.

I didn't see danger in that place. I saw protection. Even when school drills that taught us to crouch beneath flimsy desks and pretend a plank of wood could save us, I believed in that silo. It stood for safety, because someone stronger was standing guard.

September that same year: the story passed down like gospel. Eleven men stayed when the pressure rose and fuel hissed into the air. They bled it off, hands blistered, lungs burning, until the missile was safe. They didn't just save technology. They saved a town. They saved the fragile hope of children who needed to believe safety was possible.

That memory still lives within me. A shield gleaming against a bruised sky, Fritz's bark echoed on the hill. A reminder that guardianship is a posture you choose, not just a place you stand.

And it was that posture I carried into the night years later, when every other shield had failed and desperation was all I had left.

$$\text{\Large\&}$$

For eight months after 9/11, I lived in suspended animation. Not the kind broadcast on televisions across the world—twisted steel, smoke, bodies falling—but something quieter, more methodical. A different kind of wreckage.

My ruin didn't come in a single day. It was dismantled piece by piece, so carefully I could almost hear the scrape of each part being pulled away. Bank accounts drained. Files vanished. Cabinets stripped bare. A marriage already reduced to dust was now a legal graveyard, and the war wasn't fought in courtrooms but in the shadows, with lies and paper cuts that bled me dry.

Month after month, we stood before a judge. He came without an attorney, representing himself, spinning story after story, lying his face off—and getting away with it. No records. No books. No trail. Not because of me, but because he kept them hidden, always another excuse ready. A flood. A fire. A file gone missing. A shrug. A smirk. And every time, the burden fell on me, impossible to prove what had been erased.

The divorce wasn't a legal process anymore. It was siege warfare. He didn't need to win in court. He just had to wait me out. Starve me of resources. Starve me of hope.

For a year and a half, I clawed for truth—motions, subpoenas, hearings—paying lawyers money I didn't have, bleeding myself dry just to keep the fight alive. But every path dead-ended in his excuses. Every motion dissolved into his lies.

And I was close to breaking.

Then came the lie.

That I had destroyed the evidence myself. That I had sabotaged my case. That I was unstable. Vindictive. Unfit.

I watched the judge's pen scratch across his pad, his face a blank wall. A nod. A flick of the wrist. A tiny gesture that changed everything. He didn't even look up. No questions. No challenge. He moved on as if my life weren't lying in pieces at his feet.

I felt invisible.

§♦

One night, too hollow to cry, I drove to the commercial building I still legally owned. The street was silent except for the hum of one streetlamp spilling a hard yellow circle across the door. My door.

I slipped the key into the lock. It wouldn't turn. I tried again, harder, my breath coming short. Nothing. He had changed it. No notice. No warning. Just locked me out of my life.

I called a locksmith, voice steady though my pulse pounded in my ears. He studied the door, then studied me.

"Doesn't feel right," he muttered, stepping back. "You got proof of ownership?"

I didn't. Not in my hand. Not then.

So I stood there in that cruel yellow light, the useless key burning in my palm, realizing he had locked me out of more than a building. He had locked me out of the truth. Out of hope. Out of any chance to breathe free.

That night, I drove home empty-handed, wheels turning in more ways than one.

What I eventually did wasn't a choice. It was the last resort.

I owned all the shares of stock in the company. Every piece. But I couldn't prove it. The courts wouldn't make him tell the truth. The law was not interested in rescuing me.

So, I stopped asking.

There was no one left to ask, and nothing left to lose.

If he wouldn't give me the truth, I would tear it out myself.

ॐ

I made a plan, and it was brazen. Reckless. A plan that could end in prison. A plan that might end in my obituary. But desperation has a way of dragging courage out of a woman who never wanted it.

ॐ

The drive was four hours of silence so taut it hummed. No radio. No phone calls. Just the thrum of tires and the hammer of my pulse. Night thickened around me, the horizon bleeding out its last light until even the stars seemed to hold their breath. I gripped the wheel so tightly my hands ached, rehearsing it over and over. Parking. Entry. The scream of metal when I hit the gas.

Fear rose in me like a tide I couldn't stop. My chest clamped down until every breath was thin and ragged. It felt like a heart attack. Like death. Still, my foot pressed the accelerator. Still, I kept going.

Closer now. The chain-link fence came into view, sagging in spots, guarding what was mine. Beyond it, the world looked ordinary—headlights sweeping past on the highway, the rhythm of lives untouched by ruin. My life had fallen off the map.

A squad car idled in the shadows, too still. I saw it. I didn't care. Maybe they were watching. Maybe they were waiting. My breath fogged the windshield as I whispered, *At least it will all be out in the open if they stop me.*

He was gone for the weekend—at the lake. That was the only reason I dared. I parked out of sight, heart slamming, and waited until after midnight. Until the last straggler from the late shift drove off until the town folded into silence.

I turned the key. The engine roared louder than I remembered. I counted to three.

And then I floored the gas.

The SUV lunged forward. Metal screamed as it buckled, the garage door crumpling under the force. The impact rattled through my bones, the steering wheel jerking like a live thing in my hands. For one suspended heartbeat, the only sound was my breath—shallow, desperate. Then came the crack of glass, the clatter of steel, the whine of twisting hinges.

I stumbled out, lungs burning, knees weak. The air inside hit me sharply: sawdust, paint thinner, the ghost of wood shavings. My shoes crunched over screws and drywall dust. Lumber racks loomed like silent sentries. Company plaques still clung to the walls, brittle as leaves. This wasn't a victory. It was a desecration. A mausoleum of everything I had poured into him, into us, now turned to ash.

The computers were clunky towers wedged behind clutter. I ripped cords from sockets, monitors toppling, glass cracking underfoot. My hands shook so badly I could barely grip the handles. I dragged each machine as if it were a body, heaving them into the SUV one at a time. Sweat slicked my palms, dust clung to my hair, and my arms screamed from strain.

By the time I slammed the hatch closed, I was shaking so hard I could barely feel my fingers. Somewhere a dog barked, distant, accusing. I didn't wait for the dust to settle.

For a few miles, I believed I had done it. I had proof in the backseat. Proof that I wasn't crazy. Proof that he had lied.

But the truth is slippery. It doesn't always live on hard drives. It can be deleted. Corrupted. Erased.

I pushed the SUV until I reached a town so small it barely showed on a map. The motel was anonymous, neon buzzing faint against the black. I hauled the towers in one by one, arms trembling, body on autopilot. I lined them along the dresser like hulking sentinels, mute and waiting.

I sat on the edge of the bed, listening. For footsteps in the hall. For sirens. For the knock that would end everything. Nothing came. Just the buzz of neon through thin curtains, and my ragged breath.

I stared at the machines. I imagined the evidence inside—emails, invoices, spreadsheets. Proof. Salvation.

Before dawn, my phone rang.

It was him.

The police had already called. He knew everything. His voice seared through the line like fire.

"You're going to jail," he screamed. "The police are coming. You broke the law. This time, you've gone too far."

Days later, the fire softened.

"Just bring the computers back," he said, voice lower, smoother. "I'll give you what you want. I'll pay support. But I need them—I can't make payroll. You've hurt everyone, not just me."

That voice chilled me more than rage ever had. Not the screaming man, but the charmer. The manipulator. The predator who wore love's clothing.

And this time, I knew better.

⁂

In all that wreckage, there was still one shield left: Rebecca.

She wasn't just my lawyer. She was my closest friend. We first met years earlier at a women's leadership luncheon—one of those stiff events with name tags and scripted smiles. We'd rolled our eyes at the same time during the keynote, and just like that, the mask cracked. By dessert, we were already knee-deep in conversation about books, justice, and the impossible balance of ambition and grace.

When everything in my world shattered, I didn't have to ask her to stand by me. She already had. We had built businesses side by side, trusted each other with everything from payroll to pain. She wasn't a divorce lawyer by trade, but she didn't flinch. Not once.

At her urging, I did something desperate. I stole the computers from the shop, tucked them into my car, and hid out in a run-down motel in a town so small most people had never heard of it. Curtains pulled tight, air conditioner rattling, I brought in a young tech—quiet, discreet—and paid him hundreds of dollars to try to crack the files. Day after day he worked, fingers flying over keys, but the screens stayed blank. Passwords buried under digital deadbolts. My bold move failed me, and I was unraveling.

Rebecca filed a motion—carefully worded, direct, a last-ditch plea for justice. If I returned the computers, he'd be legally required to deliver a full printed set of books within forty-eight hours. It felt like a bargain made with a phantom. But I held up my end.

We hauled the machines to her house, stashing them high in the garage behind gardening supplies and forgotten Christmas boxes. That night, Rebecca's husband was at the kitchen sink when he saw them—two dark shapes moving at the edge of the yard. Their house backed onto an unlit greenbelt and sat on a quiet cul-de-sac; for a few seconds the world held its breath. He called to Rebecca from the other room, and together they went to the garage because the door was still up. In those few seconds they saw two men in dark clothing break into a run and vanish into the black of the trees. No proof. No fingerprints. But the sight of them—so deliberate, so close—was proof enough for us. We always knew who it was.

The next morning, Rebecca closed her office door. Her voice shook.

"I love you," she said. "But this has gone too far. He's dangerous, and I have to protect my family."

And just like that, my last ally was gone.

The court returned the computers to him. Still, no books. No pages. No truth. When pressed, he claimed he had delivered them, but couldn't recall how or to whom. Hinted my attorney had lost them—or destroyed them. The judge, exasperated, threatened contempt if they weren't delivered within forty-eight hours.

But they never came.

I had nothing left. The tech couldn't break the codes. The court wouldn't compel the truth. Rebecca was gone. Motions became empty lifelines. I stopped answering the phone. Stopped going outside. I took long baths that went cold around me. Watched the same movies on repeat. My body stayed, but my spirit drifted somewhere numb and unreachable.

I didn't even cry. I couldn't.

I stood in the kitchen, staring at the same coffee cup I'd used for days. My hands were shaking—not from caffeine, but emptiness. I had fought for everything. Given everything. And I had nothing to show but debt and devastation.

That was the day I stopped believing justice would come.

And yet, even then, I kept clawing for some scrap of it. I hired a male criminal defense attorney in the small town where I was living— by then I'd been there more than six months, just long enough to shift jurisdiction. It forced my ex to drive three hours for a hearing, a small victory I clung to. Even this new attorney, a seasoned man who had seen the worst of crime and cruelty, sat across from me shaking his head. "In all my years," he said, "I've never seen anything like this."

ɾ●

Then—just when I thought nothing would change—an email slid into my inbox like a quiet knock at midnight.

I sat frozen for a moment, watching the little envelope icon pulse on the screen, my chest tight as if hope itself might be a trick.

I clicked it open.

The words weren't polished or perfunctory. They didn't read like small talk or obligation. They carried something else—steady, warm, unexpected. In a season when every line I read was a demand, a threat, or a dismissal, here was a voice that felt human. Alive.

Warmth threaded through the lines, loosening something in me I hadn't realized was clenched. And maybe—just maybe—it was the beginning of light finding me where I had thought only shadows remained.

Chapter 33:

The Light Found Me

Bones Beneath the Prairie
Roseann Mayer

Months earlier, in a quiet act of daring, I had created a profile on a dating site. I wrote that I longed for a man who loved his family. I wrote that I was turning back toward Shackelford County as my home again—a place where the hunting was rich, where the lodges offered promise, and where my roots still held. Then I closed the laptop, tucked the hope away, and forgot about it—like sealing a letter I never expected anyone to open.

And then, one ordinary day, the unexpected arrived. An email. Plain. Unpolished. Nothing that should have stood out.

Except it was signed with a name I would come to carry in my heart for the rest of my life. John.

It wasn't flashy. No emojis, no clever hooks. Just words that felt steady, honest. He told me he was building a lodge in eastern Oklahoma and found it intriguing that I was interested in Shackelford County and the lodges there. He said my words read like someone who had weathered storms yet still carried her roots deep in the ground.

And then there was the photo.

He stood in a tuxedo, black curls slightly tamed, holding a wide-eyed toddler in his arms—his fifteen-month-old niece. Everything I had written—*a man who loved his family*—was answered in that single image. The baby nestled against his chest.

His hands—strong, elegant—rested gently around her, and his eyes held that impossible mix: seriousness, mischief, and the warmth that doesn't need to be explained.

That picture didn't just speak.

It sang.

And I felt, for the first time, the opening bars of a new life.

We messaged a few times, then talked on the phone. The conversation flowed like a spring creek—easy, clear, with no undercurrents of pretense. He didn't ask for a selfie. Not outright. But his warmth, his words, let me know—without bravado or pressure—that he'd choose me without hesitation, because of what he'd already seen. He asked real questions about my childhood, my favorite cookbook, and what brought me joy. He told me he didn't drink, but that I was welcome to. That tiny gesture—permission without expectation—felt like sunlight cracking open a long-shuttered room. I hadn't realized how dark it had gotten until then.

The week before we met in person, John and I spent hours on the phone. His voice was warm, playful, threaded with a confidence that came as naturally to him as breathing. He was charming, strong, funny as heck—like the popular football star every girl secretly wanted but I never dared imagine would look my way. His laughter tumbled through the line, teasing, magnetic, a little bit dangerous.

He didn't tell me much at first—just that he and his dad had run a hunting business for years, that he was buying a building he wanted to turn into a lodge, and that he wanted to see how others operated theirs. Enter me. But what he didn't say was nearly as captivating as what he did.

Our conversations felt less like introductions and more like a reunion of souls—like we were old friends catching up after decades apart.

When we finally met, the reality outshone the photograph.

That Friday, after work, I swung by my friend JC's house to grab the key from under the mat—something I'd done more times than I could count. It was always there. Always. But this time, it wasn't. My heart sank. That key wasn't just access to a house. It was access to privacy, safety, a place where I could control the story.

Now I'd have to stay at the motel—the same one where John would be.

I'd been avoiding that place for a reason. My SUV was recognizable, and Albany was the kind of town where people tracked your every move like deer in the brush. Gossip swirled with a force of its own. But JC wasn't home, and the key was gone. I booked a room at the far end of the motel and asked the owner to keep it quiet.

I texted John and offered to pick him up. As I turned the corner of the building—still on the phone with a girlfriend I had brunch plans with the next morning—I saw him.

He was standing in the doorway, impossibly handsome. Dark, curly hair that brushed past his collar, Wrangler jeans that fit just right, one arm propped casually on the doorframe—cowboy style. I murmured into the phone, "I think I'll pass on tomorrow."

When I stepped out of the Escalade, he wrapped me in a big hug. It startled me, not because it was forward, but because it felt … honest. Familiar. I didn't know what I was walking into—one of his emails had been unusually forward—but in person; he was calm. Centered. Unrushed.

His motel door was open, left ajar in a gesture of transparency. I never felt pressured. Never felt like I had to perform. Inside, on the dresser, sat a single wine glass, a bottle of red, and a worn cookbook his father had written.

That's when something in me shifted.

He took a chair. I sat on the edge of the bed. And we talked.

Not flirted. Not fished for flattery. We talked. About dogs, about droughts, about the ache of regret and the slow grace of healing. About the brutal art of forgiving ourselves, and what faith looks like when all the glitter has burned away. We tiptoed carefully but completely into those deeper waters—vulnerable and steady. And all this in thirty astonishing minutes.

He told me about his past—two marriages, eleven years each. He didn't portray himself as a victim. He admitted his failures, his unfaithfulness, and his regrets. He said he had looked his former wife in the eye and apologized, deeply and without excuse. He told me he had let his sons down and carried the ache of it still.

Every alarm bell in me should have rung. Maybe it did. But I didn't run. Instead, I sat—mesmerized by his candor. His words weren't pretty, but they were real. And then he told me the turning point: that when his second marriage ended, and even a rebound relationship fell to ash, he asked God for something different. Not a fling. Not a mask. A partner chosen by God himself. A soul mate. A forever.

I looked into his eyes—clear, steady eyes that held something I hadn't seen in years. Truth. The truth only a woman who had walked with God long enough could recognize. It bypassed logic. My body knew it before my mind caught up.

Then he took my hand and said, "Can I tell you something without you thinking I'm crazy?"

He told me he'd been praying for months—for God to send him someone to build a life with. Not a fling. Not a fix. Something real. Something better. Something that could hold. Something forever.

Before I could stop myself, I said, "I know who you are in Christ."

The words startled me, but not him. He smiled—warm and sure, like someone who had been waiting his whole life to be called home by name.

And then the dam broke.

I wept—not the tidy, practiced tears I'd rationed for so many years, but a wild, sacred unraveling. It wasn't grief, exactly. Or joy. It was something holier than both. A collapse of silence. A baptism of recognition. A thousand locked doors inside me swung open all at once. And he didn't think I was crazy!

I didn't cry because of him. I cried because something eternal had spoken—and I knew the voice.

We stayed in that room for hours, just talking. He showed me photos—his dogs, his tractor, his dad. No polish. No act. Just a quiet steadiness that felt timeless, like something I'd forgotten I could want.

Later, over dinner, the wine had softened my edges, warming me with a reckless confidence. I kissed him at the table, not realizing my first cousins were sitting just feet away. I didn't stop to say hello.

That weekend was a slow unfolding—long walks, longer talks, breakfast at the Dairy Queen. By Sunday night, I was wrung out, stunned. He asked me to marry him.

I told him I wasn't divorced yet.

It had been nearly two years, and the case still dragged on. I had a court hearing the following Friday for child support modification—another slog through a system built to wear me down.

John didn't blink. He leaned back, steady as a stone, and said:

"You'll be divorced before that hearing is over."

For a moment, the air shifted. I caught my breath, half afraid to hope he was right. I wanted to believe his certainty. But certainty has a way of vanishing in the glare of a courtroom.

CHAPTER 34:

STRIPPED BARE

◆─◇─◆

BONES BENEATH THE PRAIRIE
Roseann Mayer

That Friday morning, as I pulled into my lawyer's small parking lot, the sky was bruised with clouds. Heavy, low-hanging, the sky that pressed down on your chest before a storm broke. I was running on coffee and nerves, my blouse and slacks chosen with care to make me look stronger than I felt. My hands tightened on the wheel as if gripping leather could tether me to composure.

The air was dense, heavy with heat and anticipation. It felt as though the town itself sensed a reckoning was coming.

Then I saw them: two sheriff's deputies posted outside the door. They weren't laughing or leaning on their trucks like lawmen on a slow afternoon. They were alert, taut as wires. One rested his hand on his belt. The other's eyes scanned the street like he expected trouble.

My stomach dropped.

I parked slowly, my pulse thudding in my ears. The sound of my heels striking the pavement seemed foreign, sharp, as though I were walking into someone else's nightmare. One deputy gave me a stiff nod but didn't speak.

Inside, the lights were too bright. Fluorescent, humming, clinical. The receptionist wouldn't meet my eye, her gaze fixed too carefully on the papers in front of her. And in the middle of the waiting room stood an officer, arms crossed, face unreadable, posture alert.

The air tasted metallic.

My lawyer appeared in the hallway, his expression stark and unsettled. He didn't shake my hand. His voice was low and tight.

"What did you do?"

My mouth went dry.

"Nothing," I whispered. "What's going on?"

He hesitated before answering, as if weighing whether to deliver a blow.

"Your husband called the judge's clerk. He told them you're distraught. Armed. Planning to kill him—and the judge."

The words hit like a body blow. For a moment, I couldn't breathe.

Distraught.

Armed.

Murderous.

Me?

I wanted to laugh at the absurdity, but no sound came. My throat closed. My hands shook. The lie was grotesque, but the way everyone looked at me told me it didn't matter whether it was true.

They escorted me to the parking lot. The Escalade, my one piece of armor, became the scene of my undoing. They took their time with it, methodically pulling everything out—purse, overnight bag, even the tissues tucked under the seat. They held up each item like evidence. People walking past slowed their steps, curiosity written on their faces.

I burned with shame.

They found nothing. Of course, they found nothing. Despite that, one deputy gestured for me to follow. My legs felt like lead as he led me into a small, windowless room that smelled faintly of cigars and mildew.

A deputy waited there. She didn't smile. She snapped on latex gloves, one hand tugging the cuff tight against her wrist with a sound that made me flinch.

"Strip down to your blouse and slacks."

Her voice was flat, practiced. I did as I was told, unbuttoning my jacket, removing each layer until it felt like pieces of myself were being peeled away. Every fold was inspected with clinical detachment. My skin prickled with humiliation.

I stood trembling—not from guilt, but from the sheer unreality of it all. I wanted to scream: I am not who he says I am. But silence was my inheritance, and silence was all I managed.

Of course, they found nothing.

Two deputies flanked me, one on each side, and walked me across the street to the courthouse. Their boots struck the pavement in rhythm with mine, a steady, echoing cadence that sounded like a drumbeat of accusation. I kept my chin high, but inside, everything sagged. It felt like a public march of guilt.

Inside, he was already there.

My ex. My accuser.

He sat with his hands folded loosely, a crooked grin tugging at the corner of his mouth. He looked at me as if to say: Checkmate. The look of a man who believed the game was over, that he had won.

The judge, a well-known Baptist Sunday school teacher, furrowed his brow when he saw me. His eyes carried discomfort, but protocol forced his gavel hand steady. Procedure over humanity.

And me? I was the offering. A sacrificial lamb under the harsh glare of manufactured shame.

My face burned, a furious rush of disbelief and fire crawling up my neck. My throat tightened, strangled by the sheer injustice of it.

I may as well have been naked. Their accusations, the search, the quiet humiliations—each one had stripped away another layer. My soul felt flayed, raw, defenseless. They had ripped open every wound I had tried to stitch shut and spread it out for strangers to inspect.

And the worst part was him—watching me with quiet satisfaction, eyes gleaming with a predator's triumph. He had orchestrated my undoing, and he knew it.

The darkness in that look would stay with me forever.

I wanted to scream. To claw the smugness off his face. To rise and shout: This is not who I am. This is who he wants you to believe I am.

But I couldn't.

The silence that had once kept me safe now shackled me in place.

So, I sat.

And then, five minutes later, I broke. The sobs came—furious, unstoppable. Years of holding it together unraveled in front of everyone.

I turned to my lawyer, my voice raw.

"Get it done. Today. I'm done."

And he did.

By four o'clock, the judge granted my divorce.

It was over.

Not tidy. Not perfect—loose ends dangled, and I'd later regret some of them—but the marriage was dead on paper.

I had my maiden name back.

I was free. Or at least, untethered.

❧ Interlude—The Drive North

I left the courthouse with the taste of metal in my mouth, as if shame itself had a flavor. My blouse clung damp to my back. The air outside was heavy, the kind that makes you want to run but drags at your heels all the same.

I turned the key, and the Escalade roared to life. The deputies' shadows lingered in my rearview mirror, but I refused to look back. I had been searched, stripped of my dignity, humiliated—but not erased.

The highway opened before me, long and ribboned through fields of mesquite and prairie grass. I pressed the accelerator as if speed itself could peel me free. The sky stretched wide, bruised with storm, yet broken in places where sunlight spilled through—patches of gold laid out like a promise.

Mile by mile, the courthouse shrank behind me. The lies shrank. The predator's grin shrank. The voices that had pinned me down dissolved in the wind.

I rolled the window down and let the gusts whip my hair into a wild halo. The sound was fierce, cleansing. I wanted the road to scour me raw, to carry away the residue of that room, those eyes, that search.

Somewhere between one county line and the next, I realized: I wasn't driving away anymore. I was driving toward.

The radio hummed low, but I hardly noticed the songs. My prayer was the steady thrum of tires on asphalt. My Amen was the wind.

By the time the Oklahoma hills rose in the distance, the weight on my chest had shifted. Not gone. But lighter.

I whispered into the empty car, as if God were leaning over the console beside me: "Don't let this be another mirage. If this is you, let me know."

The horizon widened, pale blue stretching into forever. And I drove on.

CHAPTER 35:

COVERED IN LOVE

— ◇ —

BONES BENEATH THE PRAIRIE
Roseann Mayer

By the time I pulled into eastern Oklahoma, twilight had already settled across the hills. The courthouse felt a hundred lifetimes behind me, though its sting still pulsed beneath my ribs. The day's humiliation lingered like a bruise you forget until you breathe too deeply.

The small towns I passed were quiet, lights glowing in farmhouse windows, steeples etched against the fading sky. Life here moved at a different rhythm—slower, steadier, untouched by the storm I had just come through. And yet, instead of feeling out of place, I felt drawn. The road hadn't just carried me away from something; it had delivered me to the edge of something I didn't yet have words for.

I parked, hands loose on the wheel, my body still vibrating with exhaustion and anticipation. This wasn't certain. It wasn't even peace. But it was possibility—and for the first time in decades, possibility felt like enough.

John had made dinner—grilled steaks, real linens on the table, his mother's silver candlesticks catching the light. But when I pulled into his driveway, I felt a jolt of uncertainty.

The gravel crunched beneath my tires. The porch light flickered above a screen door hanging slightly askew. The yard was patchy, with more weeds than grass. The window trim bore the faded paint of too many seasons passed over. It wasn't rundown—just lived in. Frayed at the edges, like an old denim jacket still carrying the scent of every campfire it had ever known.

I sat there with the engine idling, my hands clenched on the wheel. This was not the house of polished wood and crystal chandeliers I had been raised to admire. This was not a house scrubbed into silence by appearances. This was a man's house—plain, unpretentious, a place that said what you see is what you get.

For a moment, panic fluttered within me. Could I really cross this threshold? After everything I had just endured, did I have the strength to begin something that looked so startlingly ordinary?

But then I saw him. He had stepped out onto the porch, framed by the glow of the light, waiting—not impatiently, not nervously, just steady. Like he'd known all along I would come.

Inside, the house was a quilt of small rooms and add-ons—part original, part clapboard cabin—stitched together with care, if not much money. The linoleum curled at the corners in the kitchen. Light switches didn't match. A fan in the corner clacked with every slow revolution. The couch sagged just enough to tell you it had held a thousand weary evenings.

And yet, there was order here too, though of a different kind. The kind born not of appearances but of care. Boots lined up by the door. A Bible resting on the end table. A quilt folded neatly across the back of a chair.

I had never stood in a space so far from the world I'd grown up in. It wasn't judgment—it was something else. Something startled me. I'd been raised where baseboards were scrubbed with toothbrushes, silver polished before guests arrived, where appearances were currency. Here was something different. Honest. Un-curated. Life in full view with no thought to how it looked from the outside.

John didn't know what I'd come from—did not know the invisible line I'd just crossed. I stood there in my tailored jeans and expensive boots, feeling the gulf between us stretch wide and open as a prairie—unguarded, impossible to cross without courage.

On the table, he had laid out dinner as if it mattered. The steaks were seared dark at the edges, the smell of char filling the room. There were baked potatoes, split open and steaming, butter pooling in the craters. A salad sat in a wooden bowl, cucumbers and tomatoes from his garden glistening with a drizzle of oil. And there, in the center, were two silver candlesticks, polished bright. His mother's.

It was imperfect and enveloping all at once.

I sat down slowly, my hands trembling in my lap. We exchanged pleasantries, but my mind was still buzzing from the courthouse. He didn't pray out loud—that's not him—but he did murmur, almost to himself, "Thank God that's behind you." Then he glanced up and added, "And thank God you're here."

For me. That one word caught in my chest.

We ate quietly at first, the clink of silverware against the plates filling the room. He asked about the drive. I told him about the cattle, the long miles. He told me about his dogs, about fixing the tractor that week. Nothing extraordinary. Just the conversation that reminded me what ordinary even sounded like.

After dinner, he showed me around the house. Each room carried its own story: a recliner worn to the shape of his father's shoulders, a gun safe tucked discreetly in a corner, shelves lined with books about hunting, farming, faith. It was a life built on work and devotion, not performance.

The bed—a waterbed, of all things—sloshed softly in the corner, like a relic from another decade. I laughed under my breath, not unkindly. It was a sound stitched with memory, disorientation, and something else: awe.

We spent the night together. Not rushed, not reckless—just human. The intimacy felt less like fireworks and more like the first warmth after a long winter.

And in the morning, sunlight spilled through thin curtains like a promise I wasn't sure I could trust. There were no apologies in that light. Just truth.

I had carried so many ideas of who he might be, how it might feel to finally sit across from him. In spirit, he was everything I had hoped for—steady, kind, present. But as we talked, the reality of his world caught me off guard.

My life had been filled with things: fine china, two houses, a new vehicle whenever I wanted. I had never truly controlled my spending, never faced the the kind of modest living that defined his days. His life was simpler, shaped by different choices, different burdens. I was forty-seven, worn down and stretched thin by decades of loss. He was grounded, carrying his own quiet weight, yet somehow offering me a steadiness I hadn't known I needed.

I found myself both startled by the contrast and strangely comforted by it. For the first time in years, it wasn't the stuff around me that defined the moment—it was the man in front of me.

The silence between us wasn't romantic. It was ordinary. Lived-in. And I could feel the familiar edge of panic rise in me—because this was real life, not the swept-away romance I had braced my heart against.

Something in me whispered: Stay.

I couldn't imagine starting over financially—not when I'd only just begun piecing myself back together. Terror coiled in my chest. What if I were wrong? What if this was just another escape, another mirage dressed up as a miracle?

Had I heard from God—or just my loneliness echoing back?

I stood at the kitchen sink, my hands still wet, when he came up behind me. He wrapped his arms around me gently. Not possessive.

Protective. Present. Then he turned me around, looked into my eyes, and kissed me softly.

"Who just kissed you?" he asked.

"God," I whispered.

He nodded. "Yes. He brought us together. He'll make it work. Give me five years."

And I did. We did. HE did.

The days that followed blurred into something both startling and steady. We cooked together. He showed me the property he had purchased to remodel as his lodge. We walked the fence line of one of his deer leases at dusk, his dogs bounding ahead, the sky deepening into indigo. He told me stories about his father, about lessons learned the hard way, about mistakes he wished he could take back. I told him about my children, about the long ache of loss, about the silence I was learning to break.

Each word, each step, each gesture stitched something in me that had been torn wide open.

I had found love—not the gilded, fairy-tale kind I once imagined, but the kind that grows deep in the soil of truth. It was imperfect and human and holy. It made no promises it couldn't keep, but it held me. Steadied me. Refused to let me vanish.

He radiated something I had longed for all my life—not just affection, but presence. Faith made flesh. The love of a man who knew who he was in God, and knew, without wavering, that I was his answer.

In his eyes, I saw the end of a wilderness. In his arms, the beginning of a home.

❧ INTERLUDE—LEARNING TO BELIEVE

From the moment I met John, I carried doubt like a shield. He had been honest about his past, and I had been honest with myself: I was coming out of a terrible marriage where I had sworn never again. I wanted a man whose faithfulness was visible, whose name was clean, someone I could be proud of. I wanted to see him with his family and know that he loved them, and that they loved him. I know now how much that matters, how it reveals a man's heart. Had I understood that in my first marriage, it would have been the biggest clue of all—my ex's mother's quiet, seething dislike for him, the disdain that ran under every interaction. I ignored it. With John, I wanted no blind spots.

He offered me protection, not with fists or force, but with presence. Every time fear rose in me, he said it plainly: *I'm not afraid of him, and you shouldn't be. He won't come here. He won't confront me.* And I believed him, because I knew—John was a man's man. Strong, bold, fiercely protective. He would never have stood by while someone threatened me. He would have raised a gun if he had to, and I knew, even from day one, that he would lay down his own life before letting harm touch me. Coming out of a marriage where I had lived in constant fear, that kind of certainty was a revelation. It steadied me. It helped me find the pieces of myself I thought I had lost.

But it wasn't only that boldness that healed me—it was his constancy. For at least two years I was wary, studying him the way you study a horizon for storms. And over time, day after day, the weather held. His faithfulness, steady as the sun. The good name he carried, visible in how people spoke about him, in the way his father and sons looked at him. He apologized when he was wrong, even for small missteps with me. He provided what he could—sometimes it was slim pickings, but I never had to wonder if groceries would appear on the table or if the house payment would be made. He worked hard. He was solid. And when he said he loved me, I believed it, because he showed it.

Still, we were not without fault. We have failed each other at times—wounded each other in ways we wish we could take back. My own sharp edges, his own missteps. But even in failure, there was something different here: we came back. We told the truth. We forgave. And in that rhythm of falling and mending, our love grew more real, not less.

Every morning, before I woke, he read his Bible. Never once did he use it as a sword against me. He loved my children as his own, never making them feel they were less. He cherished me, honored me. With him, there was no need to perform, no stage to keep up. It wasn't one moment that changed me; it was the gradual gathering of days, one upon another, like stones stacked until you see they've built a wall strong enough to lean against.

Even now, after more than twenty years, he laughs that I still struggle with always needing to be right. It's a reflex, a scar from the past. But when I am wrong, I admit it. And I am learning to be softer. The fire of rage was gone, replaced by the steady warmth of love. Yet warmth alone didn't fill the cupboards. From the very start, life pressed hard against us—not for lack of love or faith, but because of empty pockets.

It wasn't easy. We were strapped. There were years when the work felt endless, when we built our life on nickels and prayers. But

I learned how to work alongside him, shoulder to shoulder. He asked for my hand for five years before I finally said yes. And when I did, we built not just a marriage, but a future. By the end of those five years, we were on the road to success—not rich, not gilded, but secure.

Looking back now, I see that John and God were right all along. Trust was not a gift I handed over quickly. It was something he earned, something I allowed myself to grow into. And in the end, love didn't just give me safety. Loving him gave me back myself.

And with that return, I was ready to build a life—not just a refuge, but a world of our own.

Chapter 36:

Becoming

Bones Beneath the Prairie
Roseann Mayer

The lodge was more than a business. It was a world John and I built together—a world no one, least of all me, could have imagined I would one day inhabit.

When the season opened, and the trucks rolled up the drive, it felt like a family reunion.

Seventy percent of our guests returned year after year, drawn back by the thrill of the hunt and, more than anything, by John.

He was a guide people never forgot. Bigger than life, swagger in his walk, volume in his laugh, stories tumbling out of him until everyone leaned closer. Men admired him. Women adored him, flirting without shame, and he dished it right back. But it never unsettled me. His love was steady—a pat on the thigh under the table, a kiss on the crown of my head, the brush of his hand down my neck as he passed. I never had to wonder.

While John led hunts in the field, I worked in the kitchen. Cast-iron pans hissed, bread rose, roasts turned golden, and I set the tables with firelight and care.

When the hunters came home at dusk, our two worlds merged. Boots stomped onto the porch, voices tumbled in, and the lodge swelled with energy. We gathered not at scattered tables, but at one long one, shoulder to shoulder, plates passed down, glasses refilled again and again. It wasn't just a dining room; it was communion.

Those meals were the highlights of my day. Stories spilled as though we were kin—confessions, jokes, truths laid bare in the glow of firelight. Laughter circled like sparks. Once, a guest sloshed his glass so wide the man beside him quipped he'd "rather drink it than wear it," and the entire table roared until tears ran. Those nights reminded me that food wasn't only sustenance; it was belonging.

Through it all, John cherished me. In his bigness, I didn't disappear. I became.

One night after the plates were scraped clean, and the guests had gone to bed, I stepped outside. The lodge behind me was quiet, the laughter folded into memory for another day. Before me stretched the plains—wide, endless, starlight scattered like salt across a black sky. A breeze stirred the mesquite, carrying with it the smell of earth and fire.

And then it came—as so many memories had before—in Kodachrome slides. Bright in some places, faded in others. I saw the courthouse square in summer light, parade floats rumbling down Main Street, ticket stubs clutched in my hand. I remembered the sound drifting across town, impossible to escape, threading itself into every Albany season.

And then I heard it. Faint. Bright. Impossible.

The calliope.

Its notes rose high and wild, tuneful and unruly, floating over the plains like memory itself—shrill, joyful, alive. Built in Albany from oilfield scraps and a salvaged boiler, it was rare, dangerous, one of a kind. That sound had always been part of Albany—ushering in the parade, ushering in the Fandangle, announcing that something was about to begin.

And now it had found me again.

I wanted John to hear it too, to stand beside me and feel that same pull. I told myself it was for him, but deep down I knew: it was for me. I needed to walk back into Albany—head high, steady, alive. Not as the woman who left in fear, but as the woman who had been remade.

With the calliope singing across the dark plains, I knew: I wasn't finished with Albany. And maybe Albany wasn't finished with me either. Yet even as Albany called me back, life with John was calling me forward—stretching me past the borders of anything I had imagined—into landscapes I'd never dreamed of, challenges I would have sworn I could never face.

Some of them were small, like the crack of a rifle against my shoulder. Some of them were vast, like standing on African soil for the first time. Each one asked the same question: would I keep folding inward, or would I stand and breathe and claim my ground?

❧ Interlude—Africa

I never dreamed of Africa. I never dreamed of rifles, either. Guns had always made me flinch, even the crack of a .22 echoed like danger in my chest. The sound alone was enough to make me cower. When John offered me one, it was just that—an offer. He never pressed, never asked me to do it for him. It was always my choice, mine alone.

One summer, when a group of prairie dog hunters came through camp, I surprised myself. I went along. John handed me a long-barreled rifle chambered for .22 shells, showed me how to steady it, and told me to breathe. My hands shook, but no one hurried me. When I finally pulled the trigger and saw that I had hit, something shifted. It was more than aim. It was a release. A crack in the old fear.

John had hunted in Africa since 1978, long before Rhodesia became Zimbabwe. His stories were threaded with dust and savanna light, lions at dusk, the low rumble of elephants. They were enchanting and dangerous all at once. His group of hunters wanted to go back, and of course he wanted to return, too. One evening he asked me plainly, "Do you want to hunt, or just tag along?"

I hesitated, then surprised myself. "Maybe I'd like to hunt."

He nodded without pressure, as matter-of-factly as if we were planning supper. "All right then," he said. "I'll get you a rifle that's small, with little recoil, something that will help you harvest game successfully."

When John bought me a .308 with a recoil stock, I nearly gave up at first. The kick bruised my shoulder because I didn't yet know how to hold it close. But little by little, I found my rhythm. I learned to hug the rifle in tight, to breathe with it. One day I realized I wasn't afraid anymore. To my astonishment, I loved it—the woods, the deep red canyons, the savanna, the stillness of waiting, the fierce intimacy of harvesting what would feed so many.

John's father was proud of me—not politely, not conditionally, but with joy that spilled over. He wanted us to call him on the satellite phone from camp to tell him what I had harvested. He bragged to anyone who would listen about his daughter-in-law, the hunter. I had always been the child who had to perform for praise, but here was a man who named my success simply because it was mine.

And nothing was wasted. Every morsel of meat fed someone— ourselves, the camp staff, the villagers. Hides were tanned, bones repurposed, nothing discarded. We were hunting older animals past their prime to make way for the young. This was not just hunting for sport. This was conservation—land, people, and wildlife held in balance.

In thirteen of the last seventeen summers, I have walked the red earth of South Africa with John. Africa was not just his passion—it was his gift to me, the best of himself. On that land his love was unmistakable. He was at home there, steady in the wild expanse, alive in a way that left no doubt that this place had claimed him.

And in time, Africa steadied me too. The woman who once trembled at the crack of a rifle found herself strong in that vast landscape, harvesting not only animals but courage. Africa gave me back what I thought I had lost: the right to stand in my strength, the right to hear someone say, *I'm proud of you,* and the right to believe it.

❧

But love is not a one-way offering. Just as I had stepped into his beloved Africa, I longed for him to step into mine. I wanted John to feel my ground beneath his feet, to see the prairie light with his own eyes, to know that my roots ran just as deep as his. Albany was my Africa. The Fandangle, the Hereford sign, the bones beneath the prairie—they were my inheritance, my proof of place. And I wanted him to belong there with me, the way I had learned to belong with him half a world away.

CHAPTER 37:

PRAIRIE LAND, MY ANTHEM, MY HOME

BONES BENEATH THE PRAIRIE
Roseann Mayer

We were headed to Albany. It was Fandangle time—the first one John and I would see together as husband and wife, the first time I would take him back to the place where my story had been written long before I met him at the Beehive. Africa had been his gift to me, but now it was my turn. My chance to lead him home, to let him see my roots laid bare under the lights of a summer night, to feel the bones beneath the prairie that had shaped me.

The highway into Albany sneaks up on you. Miles of scrub and barbed-wire fence unspool like a film reel you've watched too many times. The land rolls just enough to make the horizon tilt and steady again, the way your stomach does on a slow-moving train. Then, almost without warning, the first rooflines appear—low, familiar—and there it is:

Albany, Home of the Hereford.

The sign is the same as when I was a child: weathered green, bold white letters, the proud outline of a bull. My throat tightened at the sight. Not from grief, but recognition. It was like spotting an old friend across a crowded room—one who knows your secrets and your scars and waves you over anyway.

John reached for my hand without looking away from the road. "You okay?"

I nodded. "Better than okay."

The window was half-open, letting the faint sweet smell of summer grass slip in.

Albany at dusk is its own theater. Porch lights blinked on. Shop windows glowed—each one dressed as a scene from the town's past, settlers and cowboys posed in paper costumes, a scrapbook brought to life. BBQ smoke curled from giant smokers under the trees, drifting low and slow as if time itself had paused. The scent enveloped us before we even parked.

Laughter carried across the courthouse lawn, where long tables sagged under plates of brisket and beans, Styrofoam bowls steaming, pickle spears gleaming in lamplight. Somewhere in the crowd, governors and ranch hands, oil barons and teachers, stood shoulder to shoulder, talking over the scrape of forks on paper plates and the clink of Coke bottles.

Its bright, tinny notes tumbled into the summer air like a memory you didn't know you'd been saving. It was the calliope. Steam curled from its pipes, each note a hymn, a summons. My chest tightened instantly.

"Roll it down," I told John. I wanted the sound all the way in.

The joy hit hard—chest, throat, eyes. Not nostalgia. Not longing. Bigger. It was gladness in every cell, the kind you feel at three years old on Christmas morning, before you know what it means to lose.

We parked by the Fandangle grounds. The amphitheater rose from the hillside as if it had always been waiting—stone terraces carved into the slope, the stage a sweep of emerald green. And above it, the courthouse glowed in the last light, its clock face luminous, keeping time as it had for 150 years. The courthouse wasn't a backdrop; it was the heartbeat—the one unshaken witness to every generation.

I had come searching for more than the show. I had come searching for roots. For Bette and Sandy—my neighbors from birth through eighth grade, the quiet, steady girls who had anchored my childhood.

We found each other quickly, as if the years had never separated us. We hugged in the middle of the crowd, decades collapsing in a breath. Bette's perfume carried the faint powdery floral I remembered from junior high. Sandy's laugh—soft, contained, familiar—broke loose once before her smile settled quiet. We spoke little, not of lost years, but of this night, this place. Their presence grounded me. For a moment, I wasn't just visiting Albany. I belonged to it again.

The folding chairs sat in neat rows; children raced through the aisles; teenagers leaned into each other with elbows and whispered jokes. Programs crackled in our hands, newsprint sharp and faintly metallic. I scanned the cast list the way I always had, marking familiar names, picturing children of friends stepping into roles once held by their parents.

Then I turned the page.

My mother. Side-saddle, maroon-trimmed pink velvet, ostrich-feather hat high and regal. The photograph filled half the page. My breath caught. Not from sorrow—from recognition. From the sense that memory itself had crossed the distance to sit beside me.

The lights dimmed. A hush rippled through the amphitheater. Across the valley, the courthouse glowed in a sudden spotlight—its clock visible from every seat. Time itself keeps watch. A drumbeat began, low and steady, and then the horsemen thundered in—flags snapping, hooves pounding, dust spiraling gold in the light. The crowd roared. You could feel it in your chest.

Down the hill, the side-saddle ladies followed, skirts fanned, posture regal. Then the settlers rolled their wagons in with grit and dust-streaked faces. Dancers circled to the drum, songs weaving laughter, sorrow, and the will to endure.

I leaned forward. I saw the four-year-old me: feathered headband slipping, clutching a papier mâché cactus bigger than I was, walking solemnly down the hill, heart racing as the applause swelled. That girl still lived in me, and here, in this amphitheater, she rose again.

The saloon girls strutted in feathers and fringe, voices belting. Cowboys slapped hats to their knees in rhythm. Dust, sweat, and song fused into one long pulse of belonging.

The Fandangle wasn't just spectacle. It was the town telling itself its own story, folding past into present until you couldn't tell where one ended and the other began.

৪♦

And I knew what was coming. Every year it builds to this—not just a finale, but a benediction, a song that holds the town together and calls us home.

And then—the swell, the crescendo. Prairie Land.

The stage filled with every performer, voices rising like a river in flood, surging past the mesquite, past the limestone hills, past the edge of the sky. An anthem. My anthem. The same hymn that had carried me through my mother's funeral, and later my father's—now rising here to carry me home.

They sang of wide skies and unbroken plains, of roots driven deep and courage that refuses to bend. The sound wrapped itself around me, fierce and tender all at once.

I sang too. My voice broke, tears burning hot and unstoppable— not delicate, not polite. They came from a place older than memory. It wasn't grief. It was reclamation. A summons. A naming.

That song spoke to the barefoot girl who once stood in the dust here, and to the woman beside John, who had walked through fire to return. It gathered every version of me—the child, the daughter, the survivor, the wife—and bound them to this land, this heritage, this unbroken prairie.

&

His hand found mine. Warm. Steady. The grip that didn't need to prove anything.

And in that moment—under the mesquite-scented night, the courthouse clock glowing above us, the calliope's last bright note curling into the dark—I knew the truth:

I wasn't just at home in Albany.

I was home in myself.

The music faded, the prairie night settled back into silence, the crowd drifting toward their cars. But inside me, something kept singing. The anthem was no longer only about Albany or the Fandangle—it had become about survival, about return, about unearthing what was buried too long.

For years, I thought the story ended the night I finally walked free. But freedom was only the surface. True healing lay in digging deeper—brushing the dust from the girl beneath the prairie, letting her rise into the light again.

And so the music ended, and the night was still.

But the song remained.

Chapter 38:

Bones Beneath the Prairie

Bones Beneath the Prairie
Roseann Mayer

I sit here on the beach in Mexico with John, waves folding against the shore, the light turning gold on the horizon. The air is warm; the dogs are curled at our feet, and I can feel the quiet settling into me. This is where I write the last words of this book—a love letter to the girl I once was and the woman I have finally become.

For so long, I thought I had to bury her. The girl who stayed. The girl who prayed harder, bent further, tried longer. The one who folded laundry with precision, who measured moods before setting down a plate, who practiced smiles in the mirror until they looked believable. I thought survival meant erasing her.

But she was never the problem. She was at the beginning. The bones beneath the prairie. She kept me alive when no one else could. She whispered *keep going*, when I couldn't hear anything else. She tucked notes into lunchboxes, hummed at the sink, hid small bills in her purse, and never stopped rehearsing freedom. She wasn't weak. She was waiting.

And one day, she left. She reached for the doorknob. She packed the bag. She said no. She didn't vanish. She became me.

If I could reach back—not to warn her, not to rush her, but simply to sit beside her—I would hold her hand. I would whisper: I know. I see you. You were always worth saving.

I still want to tell her: You are not too much. You are not broken. You never had to earn love by disappearing. You were already enough.

When I walk back onto that prairie sea—under the deep blue sky, the white clouds drifting, the wind restless and free—it is with her hand in mine. Her heart leaps with mine. She is not a ghost, not a wound, but the root that holds me steady. And under it all, God is the ground, the steady Presence who carried us both here.

This book is not only her story or mine. It's both. It's all the women who ever stayed too long, prayed too hard, hoped too deeply—and then, at last, walked free.

And so I carry her still. Not as a ghost. Not as a wound. But as the root that steadies me, even here, as the tide breathes in and out. The bones beneath the prairie are not shame. They are foundation. Everything I've built now rests on what she survived.

And now, as I sit here—the ocean humming beside me, John's hand warm in mine, the dogs sighing into the sand—I know what I want this ending to be. Not a closing, but a letter sealed with gratitude. To her. To me. To you.

We made it home.

Epilogue:
Truth Endures, Love Prevails

Leaving is never just walking out the door. It begins years earlier—in the bargaining, in the rewriting, in the fragile hope that maybe this time will be different. It is swallowing fear because you believe you can out-love it, out-pray it, outlast it.

There are nights when the bag is half-packed, the keys in hand, your pulse already racing toward the unknown—only to be stopped by a soft voice in the next room, a promise that sounds just convincing enough. You tell yourself those moments are enough.

When the one you love is a malignant narcissist, leaving becomes a labyrinth. They are masters at erasing your reality, replacing it with theirs. You doubt what you saw, what you felt, what you know. You stay because you think loyalty will redeem the cracks. You stay because you've been told that leaving is failure.

I stayed because I believed his words. I defended his story even as my mother lay dying, even as my family's trust unraveled. That too was part of the pattern: to cling, to cover, to carry the weight that was never mine.

And yes, when I finally left, it wasn't clean. It was tangled and flawed. There was love elsewhere—unexpected, undeserved. Some call that failure. I call it survival.

Leaving is rarely one bold step. It's a series of small, defiant choices that add up to freedom. It's messy. It's human. It's almost sacred.

☙

After all the fire and silence, I have learned this much—truth endures, and love refuses to die.

We don't all see the past in the same way. Each of us carries his or her own memories—ours to hold, to tell, even to write, if we choose. My story isn't meant to erase anyone else's. It is the truth of the life I lived, the road I walked, the woman I became.

For too many years, silence was my cage. I kept quiet because that's what I thought I had to do. Survive first, speak later—if ever. Not because the truth wasn't there, but because I wasn't strong enough to bear its cost until now.

Writing gave me back my voice. And let me be plain: I am not a victim. I am a survivor. I am a warrior. This story is unflinching, but it is not self-pity. It is the testimony of a woman who endured and finally spoke.

Yes, there was joy. I never denied that. But silence about the darker truths was its own kind of cruelty. This book is not a weapon—it is a lifeline, for me and for anyone who has walked through fire and wondered if they could make it out alive.

I know my telling may be hard for those who lived another piece of the story. That does not make my truth a lie. We each carry what was given to us. This is mine.

৶

Healing doesn't arrive in one sweep. It comes slowly—through afternoons when the light feels softer, prayers whispered without words, laughter that sneaks in after silence.

I didn't step straight into wholeness. I stumbled. I doubted. I forgave and then forgave again. But each step stitched me back together.

The bones beneath the prairie were never what broke me. They are what carried me. They are the roots beneath the life I live now.

This is what healing looks like—not the absence of scars, but the presence of roots strong enough to hold when the wind rises again.

And beneath those roots, I know this: God's hand never left me, and His holy light never dimmed. It was always before me, always showing the way forward, just as His Word promises.

৶

And may the wind that once bent me now steady you, carrying you toward the life that was always yours to claim.

Rooted, Like The Bones Beneath The Prairie, In A Strength That Endures.

RESOURCES & ACKNOWLEDGMENTS

Some books carry light into dark rooms. If you are carrying pieces of this story in your own life, here are resources that may help. These works help name the unnamable, break cycles of silence, and offer the language of healing to those navigating abuse, trauma, and recovery:

People of the Lie — M. Scott Peck

Why Does He Do That? — Lundy Bancroft

The Verbally Abusive Relationship — Patricia Evans

Violence Against Wives: A Case Against Patriarchy — R. Emerson Dobash & Russell Dobash

Above all, one book has carried me through: the Bible. I keep the Bible app on my phone so it is always near, and I read from it each day. I especially recommend the *New Spirit-Filled Life Bible* (NLT), edited by Jack Hayford—its notes and commentary have offered strength, clarity, and grounding even on the hardest days.

This memoir was not written to relive the past, but to bear witness. To affirm that pain does not have the last or defining word. That healing—however jagged—remains possible. And that the voice of survival, however quiet at first, can grow clear and strong.

To those still inside the story: there is a way through.

To those who made survival possible: thank you.

And to you, the reader—whether you came here for courage, for understanding, or for hope know this: you are not alone.

Even beneath dust and shadows, the bones still carry life.

About the Author

Roseann Mayer grew up in the oilfields of West Texas, where wide skies, mesquite winds, and prairie silence shaped her earliest sense of belonging. Her debut memoir, *Bones Beneath the Prairie,* traces a journey through silence, betrayal, and resilience to the hard-won grace of faith and finding her voice.

Though she studied English Literature and Spanish at Baylor University, she often says her real education came from the long road of life—through loss and survival, through faith and forgiveness, through discovering that the very ground that once broke her was also the soil from which she grew strong.

Today, Roseann lives in La Paz, Mexico, with her husband and their two dogs. She continues to share her story in the hope that others will find courage for their own.